*The Birth of God*

For more information:

www.treasuryofancientwisdom.com

contact@treasuryofancientwisdom.com

© A F Crowley 2019

*The right of A F Crowley to be identified as the author of this work has been asserted in accordance with sections 77 and 78 of the Copyright Designs and Patents Act 1988.*

© Jonathan Quintin
*The right of Jonathan Quintin to be identified as the artist of this work has been asserted in accordance with sections 77 and 78 of the Copyright Designs and Patents Act 1988.*

*The Birth of God*

*Footsteps Press First Edition*

*ISBN 978-1-908867-35-3*

*Reprint rights by permission of copyright holders only*

*The Birth of God*

# Contents

| | |
|---|---|
| The Birth of God | 7 |
| Ayn: Infinite Nothing | 10 |
| Ayn Sof: Nothing with no limit | 12 |
| Ayn Sof Aur: Limitless Light | 14 |
| Ehieh and the Lightening Flash of Creation. | 19 |
| The Lightning Flash | 23 |
| The Formation of the Tree of Life | 25 |
| A time to revisit and to sum up the journey. | 28 |
| The Founding of the Sephirot | 30 |
| Dimension 1 | 32 |
| Ehieh | 32 |
| Kether | 32 |
| Metatron | 34 |
| Dimension 2 | 37 |
| Dimension 3 | 39 |
| Dimension 4 | 42 |
| Dimension 5 | 44 |
| Dimension 6 | 45 |
| Dimension 7 | 48 |
| Dimension 8 | 50 |
| Dimension 9 | 52 |
| Dimension 10 | 55 |
| The Big Bang | 55 |
| Human Communion with the Tree of Life | 59 |

| | |
|---|---|
| FURTHERMORE | 72 |
| Telesma | 98 |
| The Images of the Tarot cards | 110 |
| The Life of Number Forces | 123 |
| The Eleventh Dimension | 131 |
| The Creation of Surface. God in three Dimensions of Existence | 139 144 |
| The Creation of the Physical Universe | 146 |
| The Three Key Numerical Forces | 152 |
| Atoms and Physical Existence | 155 |
| The Qliphot and Dark Forces | 157 |
| Death | 162 |
| Reincarnation | 168 |
| Birth Reincarnation and Karma | 171 |
| Revisiting the Human who Dwells within the Tree of Life | 174 |
| The Future | 181 |
| The Creation of the Twelfth Sephira | 182 |
| The Destiny of the Physical Universe and Humanity's role in Creation | 186 |
| Gravity and Quantum Reality | 196 |
| Incarnation | 201 |

## Index of Images

14 – Ayn Sof Aur

22 – Sephirot Lighting bolt

33 – Planetary Formation

47 – The names of the Sephirot

115 – The ten Tarot

119 – The Tarot families

129 – Each Sefira contains the potential to create eleven and infinity

138 – Hebrew names for the Sephirot

150 – Polygonal shapes

184 – 12 Sephirot

203 – The instant a nucleus comes into being, an infinite, holographic creation of Tree of Life matrices are propelled into being. Each Sephira contains within itself an infinite and constantly moving holographic Tree of Life creative voyage. Worlds within worlds , within worlds, without end. To go further with the holographic image would have made it incompressible to the eye.

# The Birth of God

Prologue

What existed before creation?
What existed before God?

This is not a question of faith or unfounded belief. This not a question of religious doctrine or even the limited view of modern science, which is only just beginning to stumble tentatively into the world of creation.

True science does not say "It does not exist", true science says "I, with my limited means, cannot prove it to be so, yet". True science is a never ending journey of discovery.

*Bereshith bara Elohim et hashamayim ve'et ha aretz (Genesis 1$^1$)*

This may be translated in its simplest form as: *'In the beginning God created the Heavens and the Earth.'*

This well known Biblical phrase has become so often repeated, that it has been reduced and accepted with nonchalance. But this phrase contains within it, the entirety of creation and the creative process of the physical Universe and the many dimensions beyond. It harbours the immense knowledge of the cosmos and all the possible aspects of life. These words convey that "In the beginning, God created all that is and will be in the heavens and all that is and will be in the physical Universe".

Moreover, one word alone in this phrase contains the keys to the mysterious symbol of the Tree of

Life and the hidden secrets of the creation of the physical world and of our own place on Earth. This key is the word Bereshith. It is made up of two words, "Bera" and "Shetha"; Blessed Six.

The study of the Sephirotic Tree of Life is to begin to study the unfolding of this sacred term; to study the Tree of Life is, in reality, the devotional study of the profound wisdom buried deep within this simple expression. The Sephirotic Tree is the never ending revelation of this ancient knowledge and all that endlessly continues to flourish from it.

To arrive at this moment of creation, it is necessary to search way back, beyond the beginning, beyond time itself, and begin to touch upon the essence of infinity. This is to experience the source of the creator. It is to search beyond the waking of consciousness and, ultimately, to touch upon the very birth of God.

The only possibility of deeply understanding the origins of creation, is to fuse within each stage of existence before creation; to feel and experience each infinite reality from within. The truth can only be understood by resonating within each unfolding phase of the creator, as it develops into being and by a total absorption within absolute logic, that compels each and every continual and permanent existence.

So, you are asked to put aside your own opinions, your own thoughts and internal noise. You are asked to learn, to listen and to feel. In these pages you may learn to immerse yourself in depths beyond consciousness, beyond sound and far beyond thought. You may learn the essence of logic and of all that propels existence into its continual and perfect unfolding.

You will discover the answer to the age old question, " what was there before creation and what was beyond the creator?"

You will experience the Birth of God.

# Ayn: Infinite Nothing

Endless and infinite darkness. Silence and utter stillness, beyond depth, height and breadth. No barriers, no limits, an eternal endless void. Infinite essence of non existence. Profound and limitless depth and breadth of anti–creation; non–consciousness, containing, without definition, the profound depth of non–existence.

Darkness beyond inertia, beyond concept and beyond time. Stillness, in perfect absence and perfect, eternal silence.

The absolute. The constant void.
The infinite; the eternal.

The forever dark nothingness of infinity.

# Ayn Sof: Nothing with no limit

Buried beyond comprehension, an infinitesimal and imperceptible single nano-second tic, within the infinite sleep. The nano-second tick buried in non-existent form, compels its own polarity to awaken. The dimensionless essence of non-creation; eternally within the void.

This eternal constant, lays forever, a part of the infinite void.

The fleeting imperceptible tic compels a subtle and impenetrable movement within the utter darkness. An eddy flutters within the face of the deep. Movement has not the possibility of dispersing within the limitless void and so gathers momentum.

# Ayn Sof Aur: Limitless Light

Movement against stillness, gathers
force and becomes friction against
the infinite empty darkness.

Friction creates a climax in ignition.
The constant implosion and
infinite birth of eternal light.

Eternal Light within Eternal Darkness, born of
the essence of stillness and the non creation.

The infinite light has no limit and cannot
disperse, having no boundaries within eternity.
The light is compelled to gather momentum,
drawing forever into itself; forever faster. A
gradual eternal vortex of light is whipped
into being, within an infinite womb of
light. The frequency gathering speed and
perfection. A perfect vortex of constancy.

Ehieh /I am, I will be.

The vortex of light spins with a force,
beyond comprehension, creating at last,
a unique and perfect instant of illusion;
the quintessential point of light.

This both fleeting and eternal moment of
perfect and absolute light, is the instant
of being. Consciousness. The moment
of awakening. The continual awakening
and the infinite Birth of God.

An instant of exquisite consciousness.
An emissive instant of recognition,
forever suspended in infinity. The
silent moment of "I will be."

All that was, is and will be, each unfolding,
forever bound in a constant and eternal state.

## A Pause For Thought

Each Hebrew word has been arrived at after countless years of meditation, thought and discussion by the sages of esoteric knowledge. Every word in Hebrew is created letter by letter. Each letter carries within it a numerical force of creation. The depth concealed within each word requires a life time of study and is a constantly unfolding voyage of discovery.

These explanations of the words Ayn, Ayn Soph, and Ayn Soph Aur, are a description of the states of the Creator before coming into being and up to the instant of the creator's awareness of being.

Ancient teachers contained this knowledge in simple symbols.

The symbols in themselves are unable to portray existence without limits or barriers.

Read this chapter many times, in order to begin to absorb the non-reality of the creator and to begin to understand the process and moment of naissance.

The natural question is "what caused the moment of Ayn Soph?" that infinitesimal "tic" within the darkness.

Ayn, limitless nothing, is the expression of "non-existence". By its own "non-existence", the recognition of its polarity "existence", sleeps. "Non being" cannot be, without the polarity of "being." It cannot be, without the recognition of non-being.

Because there are no limits (and much further in the process, the eternal infinity reflected in our own physical Universe), creation is caused by implosion and cannot be caused by explosion. It is impossible to explode "outside" infinity, as there are no barriers or limits.

These phases, before creation are beyond time and the process of physical creation. The process of Ayn, Ayn Soph and Ayn Soph Aur describe the formation of the primal vortex of light, that will many times be repeated until the physical Universe is brought into being.

It is vital to understand that all these phases, including our own reality, perpetually exist. The biblical phrase "I am that which was, is and will be" describes this. The past, present and future are all constant, simultaneous and eternal; existing independently and all at the same time, forever and without end.

Our own Universe is situated within a vortex of light. But not at the largest end. It is formed at the smallest point; a replica of the spinning vortex of energy that caused the very Birth of God. This is why the Universe can continually expand; because the source, the source of light itself, is infinite, therefore the result, our own recognised Universe, can continually expand.

The symbol of the sages, the point within a circle, shows us what would be seen looking from the creator's perspective down a cone or vortex of light. A vortex, spinning so fast that it appears to create a result, or point of absolute light, that appears to be stable. Our own planet appears to be stable from our perspective, but is spinning in space.

The formation of physical reality is far away. Each stage that these pages will go on to describe will express the gradual, logical unfolding and condensing of light energy, which will result in our perception of physical existence. There is no "plan," only the perfect and infinite unfolding of pure, poetic and astoundingly beautiful logic.

The formation of the first vortex of absolute light creates the illusion of the first point of existence. The first point of perfect arrival. The moment of awareness of "being" of the creator. This is the recognition of "future". This is the first perception of "I will be"; the Birth of God.

# Ehieh and the Lightening Flash of Creation.

The point of exquisite and perfect light. The eternal instant of recognition, the perfection of primal awareness. The recognition of the bursting forth of unbounded energy; this is the first recognition of future.

This fleeting instant, forever suspended in eternity. The ultimate pinpoint of absolute light, a frequency so intense that its existence within the endless light vortex, creates precession. Rings of energy ripple outwards from the primal nucleus.

Flowing into the sea of light, the ripples of energy are forced to retract and draw into themselves. Each concentric vibration of energy draws into itself, to formulate its own separate frequency of being.

The nucleus of perfect light creates simultaneous precession. The first ring of energy resonates. The repercussion of the intensity and perfection of the nucleus of light, a result that is formulated in resonance and receptivity. The second ring of energy is a fusion of light and sound, the essence of etheric awareness, of consciousness. The third ring of energy is a fusion of recognition; of affirmation. The fourth energy field is a drawing in, a primeval formulation. Each phase of energy is held in infinity, forever within its own perfect vibration.

## A Pause For Thought

The word Ehieh was created to express the moment of Ain Soph Aur formulating the point of absolute existence. The word means not just "I am" but, at the same time, "I will be". This is the primal principle of "future". This is what is referred to as the first "name" of God. Say this name to yourself "Eh hé i ey" in your internal silence and you will feel the word gently resonate around the area of your heart. Say this again internally and silently, and you will begin to commune with this moment of the birth of the creator.

There is no conscious thought, other than a recognition of existence. There are no "intentions", no awareness or plans of creation. Each and every phase that comes to pass is developed through step by step phases of absolute logic. No human perception of God existed or did exist. Absolute logic dictates.

The perfect nucleus of light was described as the "name" of God, the "father" or the aspect of the "spirit" or "Divine fire" in ancient times.

The first emanation caused by precession, like a stone dropped into water, was given the name of a "sephira" or aspect of God. This represents the soul or "Divine water", the "mother" and the result of absolute light, the creation of sound. This first ripple, caused by the impact of nucleus of unimaginable light force, is formed by, and is, the receptor of the nucleus. The receptive result, the sephira, which is the secondary energetic frequency, sound, is the understanding of the nucleus, the soul's vibrational recognition and verification of existence. This is expressed by the phrase "and God saw that it was good." Light enabling its own "seeing" or recognition of existence.

The second ring of energy was explained as the effect of fire on water, the creation of the principle of primal "steam" or primal "ether" or "thought". This was described as "air" or the "son" the first logical creation, separate from God the "father" and "mother", the first result. It was to become called the name of the "Arch Angel". Not a being as it has become known in popular culture, but a force of pure thought, way beyond our own human comprehension.

The third phase of concentric energy was illustrated as "condensation" the result of the cooling of "steam." This phase was described as the "children" of the Arch Angel or "angelic hosts", a primordial concept of emotion.

The final circle of energy is the natural fusion, caused by the light precession coming up against a "barrier" of the light of a different frequency in Ain Soph Aur. This was to become referred to as the "physical" concept, or later, the planetary aspect, although this is infinitely beyond our own concept of physical reality and quite literally light years before the creation of the physical universe.

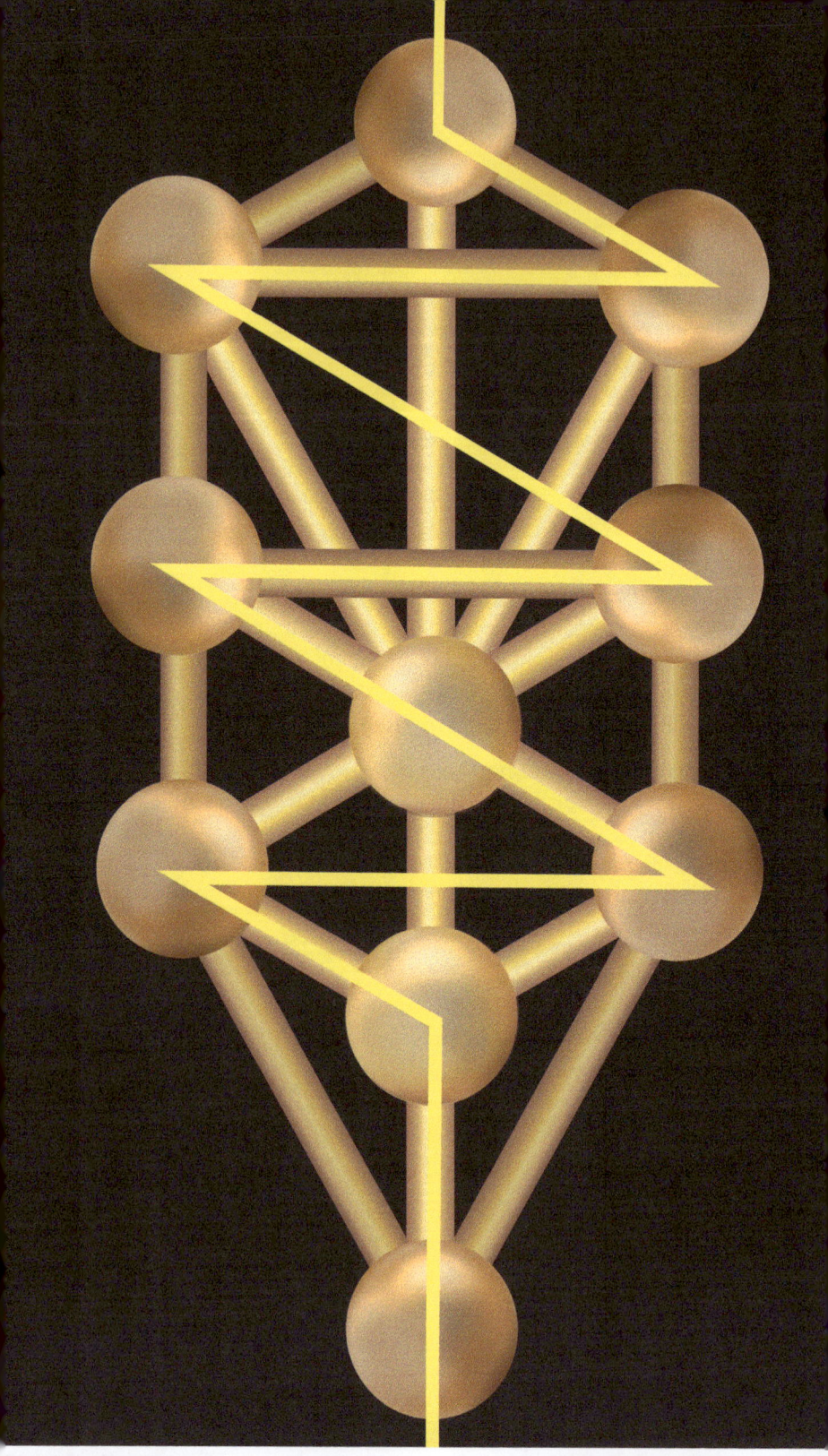

# The Lightning Flash

The magnificent exuberance of light energy
bursts forth from the first aspect of being.
It shoots an arrow of perfect, intense light
that ricochets against the illuminated sea.
The speed and intensity rebounds again
and again; a lightening flash of sublime
energy. Each contact creates another nucleus
of perfect light; each nucleus forming
instantly its own process of precession.

The divine lightening flash, forever imprinted
within the vortex of light. In a continual and
never ending process of ignition. Each point of
contact creating constant and infinite precession.

## A Pause For Thought

The immense and unimaginable force of the light bursting out from the boundary of the first aspect, unable to withhold its euphoria, creates the lightening flash. It travels with a momentum that is forced to rebound, when it ricochets against the background of the sea of light of Ain Soph Aur. The light sea is of different intensity and therefore acts a barrier. We can imagine this by picturing the action of a pinball machine. It has recently been said by scientists that atoms behave differently when they are observed. This poses many questions and offers infinite threads of thought to follow.

If we look again at the process of continual and infinite Ain, we could equate the moment of Ehieh, "I will be" as precisely this "observation." The moment of becoming, the moment of the Birth of God, is the moment of observation. Light enables us to see and to be seen. If we observe a star in the night sky, we often have an impression of the star, also being aware of us watching. The entire process of creation is an unfolding of observation; of light enabling itself to see, and to be seen. This, ultimately, will lead to the manifestation of the physical dimension.

We can understand again that within Ain, the state of nothingness can only exist because it contains within itself the recognition of nothingness. This in itself, in order to be nothing, must contain the recognition of "everything." This is the possibility of light enabling itself to see and to be seen.

# The Formation of the Tree of Life

As each nucleus of light is created, precession
follows. The force of light creates ten pin points
of exquisite light. Ripples of light ebb outwards
and draw inward, formulating ten moments
of illumination; each moment of awareness,
suspended in its own constant creation.

The immense force contained within
each aspect is compelled to burst forth
and continue its endless journey.

The first primordial Tree of Life is born,
in a perpetual state of birth. Every instant
of awareness is the consciousness of the
creator in a perpetual state of revelation; a
permanently receptive state of perfection.

The magnificent force of light energy bursts
forth continually from each aspect of creation,
reforming and restabilising at every infinite
moment. The primeval Tree of Life is suspended,
revolving forever, in the sea of light. The
receptive force is compelled to give way with
the abundance of euphoric light. The infinite
emissive source compels the shattering of each
aspect, in an exuberance of intense energy. Each
aspect reforms continually and is held in perfect
formation simultaneously, now able to echo and
continue the emissive principle of creation.

The absolute and permanent

Tree of Life is formed.

# A Pause For Thought

The emissive force itself causes what has become known as "the shattering of the vessels". This is the process of the first formation of the Sephirotic Tree of Life "shattering". This phrase has caused great concern in the past, as this has been somehow seen as a "criticism" of God. Perhaps even a comment that creation or even the Creator is not perfect. This has come about through a misunderstanding of the process itself. These two differing ideas can be brought into harmony by the realisation that our "human" idea of perfection is not in any way jeopardised by the contemplation of the process of the "shattering of the vessels". It is only our human perception that fears the idea of an "imperfect" Creator or an "imperfect" creation. If we take the time to rise above our inherited fears, we can begin to understand that in this process, lay the keys of creation itself.

The first formation of the Tree of Life created receptive "vessels" or, in Hebrew, Sephirot - the singular being Sephira. These vessels or aspects of creation were receptive due to the drawing back of energy during their formation. This primal receptivity was unable to give out or be emissive and the primeval formations or vessels were compelled to "shatter". This "shattering", in itself, was the force of emission. These aspects were then able to pour forth energy and to continue the constant creative process.

These phases are infinite, constant, and perpetual and each simultaneous stage is suspended in perfection.

The most important concept to understand, is that this entire and ancient formation is timeless, continual, simultaneous and permanent.

That which was, is and will be; all at the same time, perpetual and inseparable.

## A time to revisit and to sum up the journey.

It most important to understand that the journey so far is situated far beyond our concept of physical reality. The ultimate question of "why?" can be answered by contemplating the beginnings of this chapter. The state described as "Ayn" or "Nothing" with no limit, cannot be recognised without its polarity, of "something". Nothing does not exist, without its being recognised. Only existence can recognise non existence.

Therefore, we can express this by the simultaneous states of non existence and existence.

The expression of the infinitesimal "tic" of moment, describes that "existence" dormant within "nothingness".

We can illustrate these phases with this formula:

> NOTHING + MOVEMENT = FRICTION
> = IGNITION = FIRE = LIGHT

Limitlessness enforces this movement to gather momentum. To spin faster and faster, as there is nowhere and nothing to impede its force. The moment whips up a vortex of energy, spinning ever faster and ever more intense. Due to the immeasurable speed, a pin prick of absolute light appears to be formed. It appears to be stable due to the velocity of the spin. This moment of formation is the quintessence of the light coming into being and the recognition of "being" itself.

This phase can be expressed with

the following formula:

> IMPLOSION OF LIGHT + MOVEMENT
> = MOMENTUM = VELOCITY =
> VORTEX = EPICENTRE = BEING

We should therefore consider creation as being caused by implosion. It is impossible to "explode" when there are no limits, to explode beyond.

The apparent stability of the nucleus of light sends a message of movement, echoing and repeating the principle of movement within Ayn Soph.

The lightning flash of primal energy rebounds against the light of a differing frequency to its own velocity. Each moment of ricochet creates another nucleus and another message of momentum is set in motion.

These phases can be expressed as the purest and most primeval form of both dynamic and static geometrical energy.

The source of dynamic or mutable, concentric energy, flows from Ayn, Ayn Soph and Ayn Soph Aur. It is replayed in the formation of each Sephira. The natural process of the lightening flash, caused by the momentum of dynamic energy, is the first possibility of static geometrical force that will later formulate the possibility for physical creation.

All these phases of creation are formulated by a simple repetition of principle and steps of logic.

# The Founding of the Sephirot

The coming into being and formation of the Sephirot, the aspect and attributes of the Creator, is immeasurable and beyond description. The ancient sages of old devoted lifetimes of meditation and discussion attempting to describe this. The Sephirot; the word Sephira and its plural Sephirot have their origins in word Sepher, book and numeration. This tells us that the Sephirot are titles of immense and immeasurably profound books of knowledge, containing mathematical keys.

As each aspect of the Tree of Life bursts forth into existence, the creative force recognises its own discovery by the sensation of resonance, that reverberates from the nucleus, caused by the immense force of the vortex of whirling light energy, hurtling and ricocheting against the light of Ain Sof Aur. (The words used, 'feeling' and 'emotion' are pale reflections of these indescribable forces.)

The Creator and creation are permanent coexisting states of discovery, observation and verification; and God 'saw' that it was good.

The ignition of the nucleus of birth is observed, 'light enables us to see and to be seen', and verified by the receptive, or emotional response. Thus 'in the beginning was the word and the word was with God and was God'. This phrase shows us that the beginning was the secondary phase and that "to begin" tells us that there was a process before this 'starting' point. To verify a beginning asserts that there were both something and nothing before. This verification of existence, caused by the essence of light, can be equated to primordial sound or the word.

The moment of the flourishing of light from the depths of Ayn is in a perpetual acceptance of "recognition" and "verification" Let there be light, the primordial word "Telesma", resonates and is the receptive vessel of sound. This is the recognition of light, the "seeing" that light was good, exquisite, harmonious resonance.

The most vital and highest knowledge, is the understanding of the Holy and Sacred name of God that brings into being every nuance of existence. Each new unfolding, every direction and aspect of existence, is called forth by the name of God that is formed from the intense, focussed light of perfection.

The name of God, which can be understood by absorbing, dwelling and entering into, the physical world of light, is communed with by our sense of sight. By working with and drawing into ourselves, physical light, by beginning to breathe in sunlight and contemplating the sun, we begin to have an insight into the intensity of the light, created by the process of Ain Sof Aur, that creates the first coming into being of what we call God. The first nucleus of absolute and intense light that we call the "Name of God"; each name has been painstakingly arrived at after generations of precise and detailed observation and physical experience of the reverberation of the experience of each name coming into being.

The Birth of God is observed by the verification of light and the resonance of 'it was good'. Light creates, and sound, forms.

# Dimension 1

## Ehieh

The Birth of God

The letters chosen by the ancients combine breath, the spirit of the entirety of all that will be created, the hand of the creator and the window, or opening within light itself, from whence the light of creation constantly flows.

I am, I will be, the beyond, a constant and permanent state of birth.

## Kether

The name given to the formation of the first Sephira. The soul of creation and the first effect of light; sound. Sound, caused by the reverberation of the nucleus of light, the name of God. Here indicated by the 11$^{th}$ letter, illustrating the infinite holographic creation of perpetual unfolding and creating.

The reverberation, the emotional reception of the nucleus of light, the womb and soul, in a permanent state of receiving.

The human sense of hearing allows us to commune with this process. The first wave of receptivity, of sound and of reverberation.

The reception of cause.

The letters representing the possibility of infinite reverberation, of infinite harmony and

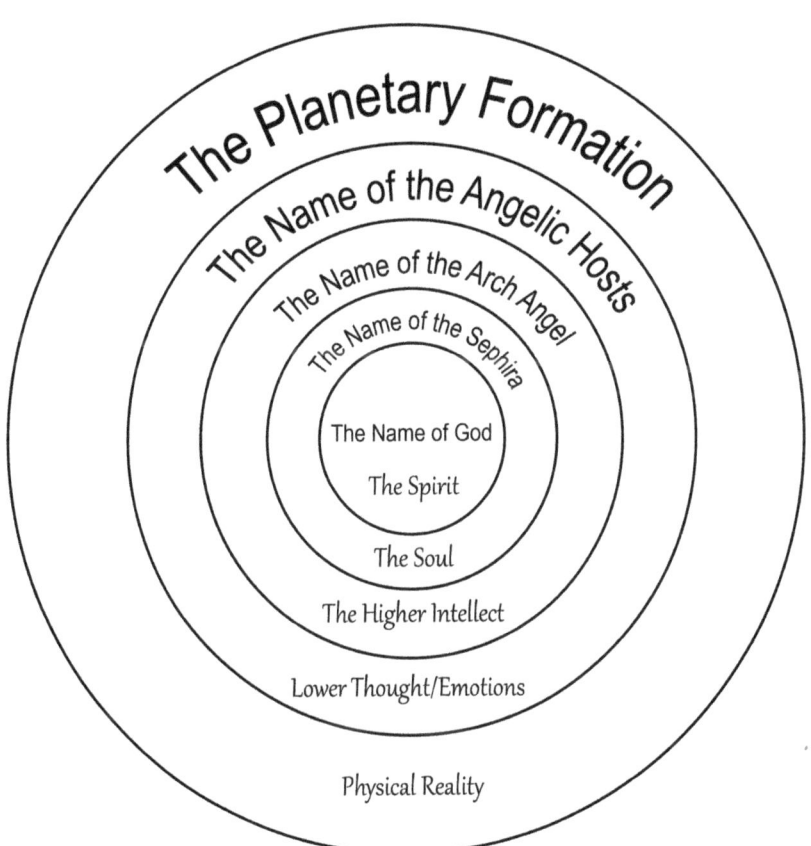

precession. The letter chosen represents the force of the number eleven, showing the holographic, infinite and constant, self regenerating Trees of Life, endlessly ricocheting into existence from the instant each nucleus is formed.

The middle letter, its symbol, the cross, indicating the physical formation of creation and the unfolding of the twenty two paths of the cross in three dimensions, the twenty two faces of the three dimensional cross, the Tree of Life.

The final letter, the symbol of the sun, upon which all physical life shall depend. The essence and embodiment of the light of the creator.

## Metatron

The co-creation and result of the emissive, 'firey' force of the sacred name of God, the Spirit (the Father) and the receptive force (the Mother or womb) of the soul, the primordial 'watery' essence of the vessel of sound and reverberation. This is the eternal 'child' of the two states of being, the result, the product.

The first force made from the fusion of the spirit and soul, the nucleus and the receptive vessel. This may be equated with "steam" or "ether", the result of fire and water. This "ether" is the essence of pure, perfect thought. Thought generated from light and sound, that is its own unique life force.

The letters of this force begin with the final
Mem, the entirety and inseparable water, from
which flows the breath of life. The force of
pure thought bursts into existence through
immense impetus of the spirit and fire, the
letter of the sun, the King of physical life,
directs the force through a constant cycle
of regeneration and perpetual rebirth.

This word, or name, of perfect thought, has
been called the 'Archangel', the first being made
of the two polarities of the creator, the nucleus,
the sacred name of God and the vessel, the
Soul and the name of the Sephirot. The word
Metatron may be understood as 'He who stands
by the throne" and has been described as the
"eyes" and "ears" of God. The eyes represent
light or sight and the ears represent hearing
and sound, the two polarities, the Spirit and the
Soul. The birth of Metatron is the verification
and response of "seeing that it was good".

This immense frequency, that is created
from and eternally draws from the source
of the firey emissive spirit and from the
mutable watery receptive soul, gathers
vibration and energy. The etheric vibration
of thought is perpetual and infinite.

This is the beginning of 'focus' upon the
verification of 'seeing that is good' the
observation and the emotional verification of
the soul, is generated and gathers momentum,
and becomes ever more of 'seeing that it
is good', focussing and creating 'good'.

This living force of thought begins to compound its essence of thought, through momentum and focus. This process can be equated to condensation, the effect of steam or 'ether', as thought flows further from its source, it becomes 'condensed'.

This is the product of the 'Archangel', the ferocious force of pure thought. The product, becoming ever more condensed, has been called the 'angelic hosts', or children of the Archangel.

These children of Metatron have been named **Hayot ha Kadosh**, or Holy Living Beings.

They are described as living in a continual state of absolute euphoria, surrounding the throne, or essence of Kether, 'the crown of the royalities who reside on the throne of light'.

The quintessence that nourishes these beings is pure and ecstatic light. These beings are eternally one with euphoric light.

Their name tells us that they are made of sacred holiness and know no other existence.

They resonate, vibrate and emit this euphoria, which emanates from them and condenses around them, surrounding them in an accumulation of energy. A swirling of light vibration, described as the 'physical' aspect, the fifth precession.

**Rashit ha Galgalim**, the first swirling, this name describes the light source which has become condensed, the pure force of the spirit and the momentum of the sacred pure light vibration. The eternal swirling quintessence of light, that suspends the inhabitance of the Creator.

## Dimension 2

The energy becomes too great to be contained within the suspension of the first Sephira and is forced to burst forth from its constriction. Momentum and vibration whipping itself into another vortex becomes focussed, creating another pinpoint nucleus of light. Another 'pebble in water', another nucleus of intensity that causes waves of light precession.

The nucleus is created by such intensity of emissive light that the sacred name 'Yah' was given to it. 'Yah', containing the yad, the holy letter that contains all the elements of creation and is the number ten, the symbol of this letter is the 'hand of God'. The three letters combine the hand of the creator and the direction of creation. In the centre of the name dwells the force of breath and at the conclusion is the feminine force, the letter He; the symbol of the window, from whence the light again eternally erupts. The sacred name of Yah, God the Father, is the embodiment of the force of emission.

The acceptance of this existence, the recognition of this birth is received within the resonance of precession. The spherical outward reverberation, caused by the nucleus of existence, the 'seeing' and 'knowing that it is good', the vessel of acceptance and emotional harmonising of the primordial soul, forms the vibrating sephirot and the name **Chokmah**, 'wisdom'.

The first letter of the name of the Sephira expresses the encompassing of energy, the central letter illustrates the divine, perfect quintessence of pure light and the ever-unfolding process of creation, followed by the Mem, the sacred water and womb of life, the last letters expressing the life force flowing outward and onward.

Chokmah, or wisdom, is an accumulation of the all that had led up to that moment; each experience, timeless and permanent.

The spirit, the sacred name of God, Yah and the name of the soul, the emotional recognition of existence, the name of the Sephira, Chokmah, create the etheric vibration of thought, their child. The name of the child, the Archangel the embodiment of the force of immense thought, is **Raziel**, the Secret of God and the force of wisdom.

The letters of this name describe the physical royal embodiment of light, the Sun, The communication of this energy through the letter Zayn, the 'sword' of perfect thought, directed by the Yad, the Hand of the Creator, harmonising in perfect equilibrium in the formation of the holy letter Lamed, the seventh day of creation, the celebration of creation. "I El", of God, the secret of God's wisdom.

The coagulation of thought further manifests the following, more dense radiation from the nucleus, the 'children of the Archangel', the angelic hosts. These are the **Ophanim**, or wheels of fire. Made of utter fire, described symbolically to have eyes that 'see' in all directions. Wheels of fire that turn gyroscopically and eternally, experiencing an infinite existence of the quintessence of the spirit, the life force itself.

The reverberation further compounds the final, fifth wave of precession and has been given the name **Mazaloth**, or Zodiac. This symbolises the culmination of thought and emotion (far beyond our human imagination and experience) the concept, set aside, for physical creation, not yet conceived by logic.

The Mem describes the womb or soul of life itself, the Zayn the force of perfect thought that will dwell within the womb, the accomplishment of the holy letter Lamed, the equilibrium and balance and the sacred Tav, the cross upon which the physical creation may be suspended, around which each phase and force may logically unfold.

## Dimension 3

The journey of light, focuses and creates the nucleus that has been described as the sacred name of God **YHVH**. This sacred name contains within it all that will eventually lead to the principal of physical creation. This is sacred name of the creator, the Mother; the feminine force of stability and receptivity to the light force of the emissive spirit.

The letters of this sacred name illustrate the four phases of manifestation from the absolute spirit, Yad, the number ten, representing the spirit and physical matter. The letter He, the Mother, Isis veiled, beyond physical understanding. The holy Vav, the symbol of the nail, the pivot point, all that secures wisdom to the unfolding cross of the Tree of Life. The Vav is the extension of the Yad, the son, the child of the Spirit and Soul, the Yad and the He. The Yad is thought. The final He is the repetition of the Mother, the physical stability, the daughter. The final He is a reflection of the process of the formation of the stable Tree of Life and the journey of perfect and poetic logic, which will manifest the physical experience of the Birth of God.

The recognition of the sacred name resonates. The Sephira has been given the holy name **Binah**. The first letter is the Bet, its symbol is the house. The Holy Yad; the creator spirit. The Nun, the symbol of the fish that swims in the soul of life, in both directions, is the symbol that embodies rebirth and reincarnation. The breath of life flows once more through the Hé, the window. The unending and eternal flow of life.

"Understanding" is the state of utter stability. Understanding and resonance, to be found beyond all experience. This is peace. Sephira Binah is sometimes referred to as the dark face of God the Mother. The dark depths of reception and utter stability.

Wisdom is all that is accumulated from the past. Understanding is all that will create the future. The reaching outward, the voyage of discovery in its primal state, the instant of recognition the sacred word Ehieh, I am and at the same time, I will be; the Birth of God. This recognition, Sephira Binah is the formulation of the possibility of 'future" and the precursor of time.

The child of YHVH and Binah is the thought force or Archangel that has been given the name **Tzaphkiel**, the Contemplation of God and formulates the essence of the divine water or the universal soul. The first letter Tzaddi, is given the symbol of the star and brings forth from its depths, the river of life. The letter Pe is symbolised by the 'mouth' of the creator, from whence sound, the Holy River Life flows. The letter Kaf, indicates the purity of Kether that has created it. The letters combine to create the word The knowledge of God, knowledge from still, stable contemplation.

The condensation of thought formulates the children of the archangel, thought and emotion, here named the **Aralim**, the thrones. These are beings of absolute stability.

It is said that all humans will one day stand before the thrones and proclaim themselves stable in the face of all stability.

The first concept of physical manifestation is now possible and given the name **Shabtai**, the force that will later formulate the planet Saturn; described as the cold of wisdom.

These three Sephirot together form the first concept of flat surface and the first building block of life.

This first triad, named **Aziluth**, is the original model from which all else is made. It contains in every conceivable way, every aspect of life and is the template from whence all creation will develop.

This word, in itself contains the Alpeh and Tav, the first and the last, Ehieh Asher Ehieh, I am that I am. Illustrating that all is simultaneous, the first and last in synchrony and constant awareness.

## Dimension 4

The energy flows downward and forms another nucleus of perfect light. This name of light is heard internally as **El**, the Ever Loving God. This is the title of the endless book of love, that flows without end, throughout every aspect of creation. This state of unconditional and perpetual giving out, is the embodiment of God, seeing that it was good.

The Sephira **Chesed** has been interpreted as Loving Kindness or Mercy.

The reception of this nucleus of perfect light resonates and forms the Sephira Chesed. The letters of this word describe the encompassing of pure love by the Cheth. The Sameach shows us, here, all is combined to the service of the world above. The word also contains the Dalet, the symbol of which is the doorway and through this doorway, its perfect energy will flow down throughout the later phases of creation.

Shakespeare's The Quality of Mercy speech from the Merchant of Venice expresses beautifully the resonance of Sephira Chesed. This is the God state of the Garden of Eden and the origin and conception of the human principle.

The name of God El and the receptive Soul create the next dimension of existence, their child, the Archangel, the perfect thought force, **Tzadkiel**, The Justice of God. This is thought force, made entirely from and incessantly emanating, absolute and constant love.

The condensation of this majestic force of love, the children of the archangel or angelic hosts, are named **Hachmalim**, the amber ones; the glowing sparks and embers of fire, made of the quintessence of love.

**Tzedek**, Jupiter, is the principle of physical creation that compounds the precession, as the waves of vibration draw back from the boundary of infinite light. The word Tzedek illustrates that justice is the creation of unconditional love.

## Dimension 5

Onward the immeasurable ignition of energy hurtles, creating the fifth pinpoint of perfect light. The nucleus that has been given the sacred name **Elohim Givor**. This is the ever generating, splitting and dividing of light, the creator becoming 'many' but eternally the one. This sacred name expresses the culmination of power and force beyond comprehension. This fifth stage is the splitting and dividing into the ignition of light, which will fuel every atom of creation.

The sacred word El, has become a transformer of immense and perfect, ever generating, love and a constant state of perpetual division. The Gimmel describes the generating of pure love, fuelled from the crown of Kether and directed and concentrated with precision. This is the primal discovery of 'intent'.

The sensation and resonance of this nucleus has been called **Gevurah**, power or strength. This is the awareness of the infinite power of the creative force; the unstoppable force of life. This is the manifestation, emotion and resonance, of the primal forces transforming into and becoming the Creator of life.

The child and result of the nucleus, the Spirit, the sacred name of God and the resonance and sound vibration of the soul. The Sephira has been called **Kamael**, the Desire of God. This immense force of thought directs and vibrates the first journey of intent, of reaching out beyond and into the voyage of creation.

The condensation of thought, the children or angelic hosts of the Archangel are described as the **Seraphim**. Firey beings, containing the essence of life. They have traditionally been illustrated with three pairs of wings, which symbolises the ability to fly freely throughout the three worlds of creation.

The final reabsorbtion and subtle formation of the fifth ripple of precession has been named **Maadim** or Mars, the principle of the red planet. Red representing the physical life force which will later come into being.

## Dimension 6

The vast forces culminate in a centrifugal nucleus; the vast exuberance of light and life itself. The sacred name born here is **Eloha ve Daath**, 'I am ever eternal love, in midst of the gateway of mysteries and ancient chaos and darkness .I am eternally light. I am eternally love'

The sound waves resonate and reverberate; forming the Sephira and soul of eternal light and perfect love. This Sephira has been named **Tifaret**, Splendour. This Sephira is a continual celebration of light. It is culminated of all that has contributed to the Birth of God. Upon this state of being, all life depends and from whence all life is drawn. This is the key, the sacred six, the sacred pattern of birth and eternal life.

The Spirit and Soul, the sacred name of God and the Sephira, create the thought force, the Arch Angel **Mikael**. This name is a question, 'Who is like unto God?' This arch Angel is a perpetual state of wonder, an eternal state of basking in the splendour of the Creator and an eternal state of amazement, suspended in the question 'Who can compare to this infinite and incessant splendour?'

The condensation of this immeasurable force Mikael, are the children or angelic hosts called **Malachim**; messengers .These forces transmit the message of supernal light and commune with the highest aspect of, what will become the principle of the integral higher nature of humanity. The higher bodies or real essence of the human consciousness is forever dwelling within Sephira Tifaret and eternally commune with the messengers of light, the Malachim.

The fifth reverberation stabilises and becomes the principle of **Chemesch**, the Sun. Humanity retraces its connection to Sephira Tifaret through dwelling upon and learning the secret practise of breathing and holding within the sun's rays. To truly understand the force and life of light, the Sun, around which the planets revolve and upon which all life depends, humanity must commune with the life giving rays of the Sun. In Sephira Tifaret, the quintessence of the original and perfect human dwells, Adman Kadmon, the spirit of humanity, the Christ spirit of every being that will one day be conceived on the Earth.

These three Sephirot form the second,

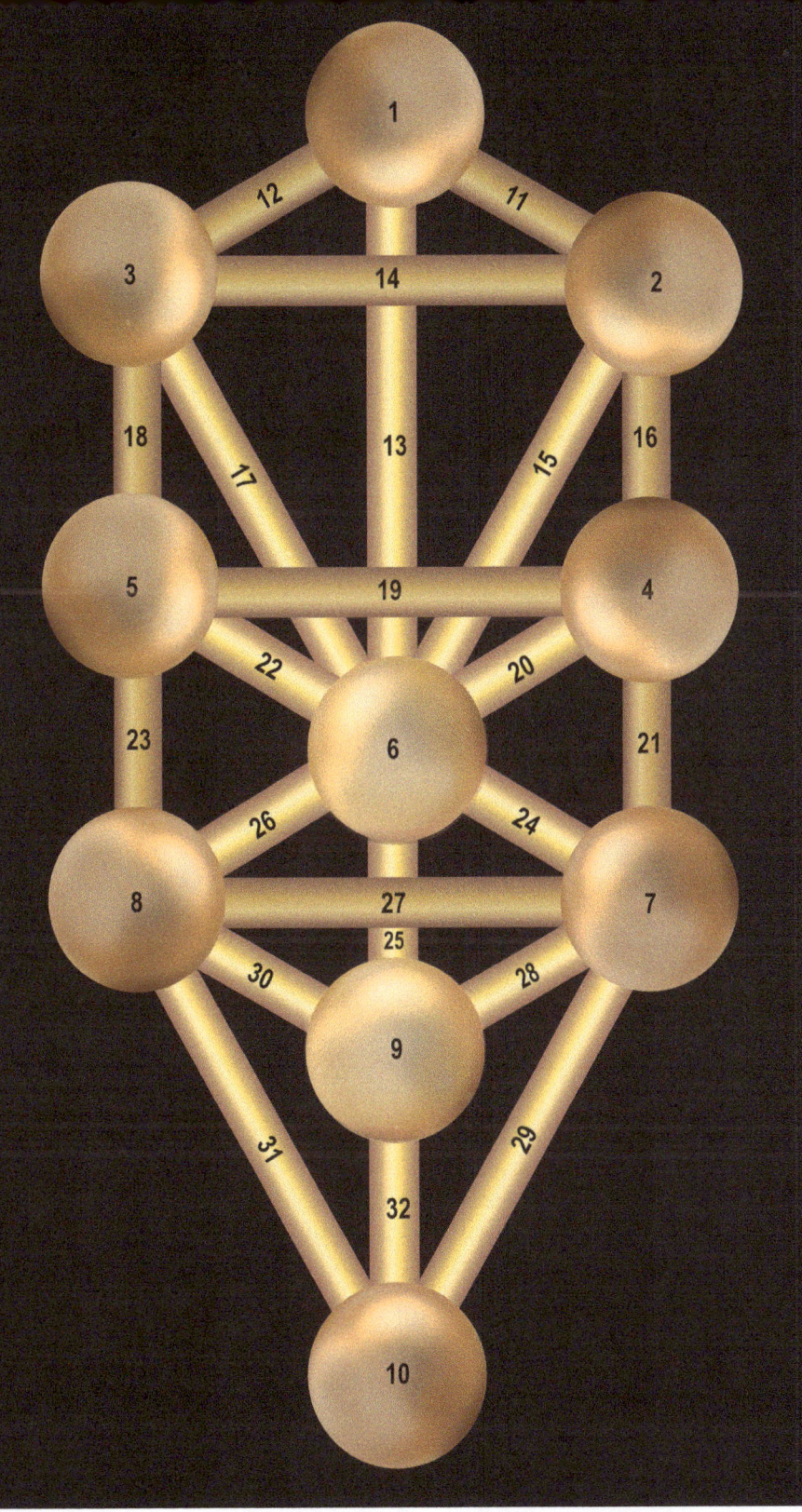

downward flowing triad, **Beryah**, the world of Gestation, the womb of life. The two triangles, the upward eternally pointing triad of the world Atziluth, the world of the spirit, combines with the downward flowing triad Beryah. The world of the Spirit and the world of the Soul, together in perfect harmony, of light and sound, creating the Holy Magan David, the Star of David, Solomon's Seal, the fusion of God the Father and God the Mother, in perpetual union.

## Dimension 7

The journey of light speeds onward. Another nucleus is formed, given the sacred name **YHVH Tzvoath**; one that has become many and is the Lord of hosts. The spirit focuses into a point of perfection, myriad possibilities of light are ignited within its self focusing. Within the letter formation we see the Tzaddi the pouring of the perfect force of life, the Holy River of Life, that will flow into creation. We see the Vav, compounding and securing the forces of life. We see the Holy Tav, the cross upon which life will harmonise physical balance.

The precession of "feeling" recognises its being, it resonates harmony. The sacred name given to this Sephira is **Netzach**, Victory and Endurance. This is two words with one meaning; the aspects exist because of each other and are interdependent. We see the process of evolution and rebirth, we see the perpetual River of Life blessing creation and the encompassing of life into the principle of physical appearance. Within this Sephira lie the dormant forces of nature, the embodiment of the two polarities which will unite to reproduce. Here lay the elements of the physical Universe and of the life we have in such extraordinary abundance on our planet.

The Spirit, the Sacred name of God and the Soul, the Holy name of the Sephira, create their child, the Arch Angel who has been given the name **Haniel**, the Grace of God and is received as the Angel of Divine Work. This is the formulation of perfect active thought; focussed and deliberate intention. The letter of this name express the window from whence the light of God shines, the beautiful and poetic flow of reincarnation and resurrection, we see the hand of God and all the knowledge of the creative process and the perfect balance and celebration of the principle of creation and of nature.

The condensation of the thought accumulates and becomes the children of the Arch Angel, the angelic hosts, called the **Elohim**, the principalities. These entities emit the great forces that will gravitate and become the world of nature within which humanity resides.

The last ripple rebounds against the light within which it discovers its existence and formulates the physical, planetary aspect. This has been named **Noga** or Venus. The letters again express the constant rebirth of what will become physical life, it shows the Gimmel, the symbol of the camel, the survivor in the desert that carries its own supply of water (the symbol for the soul). It is the symbol of astral poverty, it does not need huge and cumbersome emotional needs and can easily pass through the 'eye of the needle', the entrance to the perfect world of Atziluth above, the message of how to sustain earthly happiness and the repetition of the cycle of life. It is said that the bee was born in Venus, the planet of love and Nature. This has become the symbol of the Initiates, who have learned to rise above the torment of emotional needs and the scourge of doubt. The bee is said to die if it stings and symbolises the damage we do to ourselves by our misguided actions. Within this word lay the keys of balance and harmony.

## Dimension 8

The lightening flash of light hurtles across the space of perfect light and rebounds, the vortex of energy focuses into another nucleus of absolute and intense light. This is God coming into being in state of existence that has been given the Sacred Name **Elohim Tzvaoth**. The Holy Many of Many. This explains the blessed and holy vibration of every atom of existence. Here we can truly begin to understand the sacred life force contained within every minute flicker of life, within the One, all dwelling and depending upon the life which is God and is the continual Birth of God.

The light waves eddy outward from the nucleus, recognising and resonating its own reality. The Sephira, the Soul, has been named **Hod**, the great Window, the Great Doorway. This is the eighth Sephira and is a perfect illustration of the life flowing downward and returning to the source. This is the celebration of life. The Sephira is a resonance and a vast symphony of joy.

The sacred name of God and the name of the Sephira, create the outburst of energy that is the embodiment of thought; an exhilaration of thought, and is named **Raphael**. The first letter expresses the life giving force of the Sun; an ever giving exuberance of light and life. The letter of the great force of the letter Resh, the life frequency, the life giver, the Sun, is a glorious outpouring of health and vibrancy. The letters form to create the Healing of God, the Arch Angel who is said to plead for your joy incessantly until he receives an affirmation of an accomplished prayer.

The condensation of joy and health, the children of joy, are the angelic hosts, given the name **Bnei Elohim**, Blessed sons of God or angelic beings. These divinities, the children of joy, dwell and move in the lower etheric and astral regions and commune constantly with humanity. It is said in the ancient scriptures that there are a thousand angels caring for the evolution of every human.

The last reverberation of energy draws back into itself and formulates the physical principle of **Kohav** or Mercury; the force of communication and the physical messenger of heavenly influences into the physical plane. The symbol of Mercury combines the two polarities of the creative process and the Creator. It expresses the essential balanced exchange between the emissive and receptive qualities and forces that call creation into being.

## Dimension 9

The untamed lightening flash reaches the conclusion of its energy, formulating the last individual, primary phase of creation, the ninth nucleus. The sacred name of light has been called **Shaddai El Hai**, Lord God of the Heights; the sacred mountains. This begins with the ignition of the fire of the spirit through the sacred letter Shin. We see the Holy fire pass through gates of the letter Dalet, the hand of God, the Holy letter Yad, directing the light of the life force. We see the perpetual Love of God in the centre of the name, the last word vibrating with light, the window through which the Divine Light shines and is again directed into physical creation by the sacred hand of God.

The reverberation resonates and forms the Sephira, the receptive, feeling Soul. The name given to the ninth aspect is **Yesod**, the Foundation. The number nine is the foundation stone of life; the incessant multiplication of the soul. There are only nine numbers, nine phases. Yesod is astral region of emotion. The symbol of the pearl belongs to this dimension. The pearl is the result of the oyster working upon the irritation of the grain of sand embedded in its body. With time and perseverance it transforms it into a beautiful pearl. When we leave the earth and go through the death process, it is said that we pass through the pearly gates. This is the division between the dark and pure light side of Sephira Yesod. To succeed we must leave behind our grievances and difficulties and embrace the pure light of Yesod, to continue our journey into the source of creation. The quintessence of the pearl flows down from high above in Sephira Chokmah, the mutable and pearlescent energy of wisdom. The pearl becomes fashioned and stabilised in Sephira Yesod, by working upon and transforming our worldly cares. This pearl is of great value and 'should not be cast before swine' to be 'trampled underfoot', the lower nature of mankind and the feet, the region of the physical world, where its essence cannot be seen or valued.

The Spirit and the Soul, the sacred name of God and its bride, the Soul, the Sephira, together create the Arch Angel, the immense force of thought that embodies and vibrates the essence of its Father and Mother. This is the Arch Angel named **Gavriel**, the Power of God. The Archangel of Yesod, Gavriel is traditional depicted with a trumpet, as the Divine Herald. This thought force conveys the message of the Christ, the Divine source of humanity and its great journey of becoming a creator through the perfection of thought and feeling. The journey of vibrating in harmony with God.

The condensation of thought, the angelic hosts, convey and contribute to this destiny. They are named **Kerubim**, Angels, the divinities that accompany every human life along its path. These are the angels that lift up the downhearted, and perpetually reaffirm and delight in each human transformation. They delight and dwell in awe, as each human takes up his destiny as a child of God and begins the revelation of his own Divine power.

The last, fifth, reverberation of vibration, rebounds and draws into itself, creating the principle of physical manifestation. This is named, **Levana**, the Moon. This is the aspect of surrender. Levana surrenders its being to the illumination of the Sun and becomes a light source in darkness. As the Earth and planets circle the sun, the moon is seen throughout many phases of surrender; the waxing and the waning; the full bright silver light and rebirth of the each new phase. Levana teaches us how to understand the tides and oceans of life, death and rebirth.

This downward flowing triad forms the region named **Yetzirah**, the formative world. These are the regions of thoughts and emotions that gather the life force and momentum that creates physical experience.

# Dimension 10

The ignition of light continues and gathers momentum; the energy appears as manifest, physical 'reality', due to the immeasurable speed of creation.

## The Big Bang

The vortex of whirling, spinning light once more appears to have 'stabilised' into a nucleus of intense, perfect light. The Sacred name of God in this 'manifested' dimension is **Adonai Malek,** Lord God the King. This describes the ultimate act of creation, the manifest world, held in an illusion of physical time and is the Kingdom of life. Within this word we can see the letters that express the breath of life itself passing through the doorway of the higher dimensions, we see the ebb and flow of the process of re incarnation, we see the Divine Water, the womb of Life, we glory in the celebration of the seventh day, the celebration of creation and finally we see the Holy force of pure light , that flows eternally from the pinnacle and crown of the Sephirotic Tree, Kether.

The nucleus causes another process of self recognition, as the concentric rings of reaction eddy outward. The name of the Sephira, **Malkuth,** the Kingdom, express the resonance of the soul, feeling its existence. The last letter Tav, the symbol of the cross, expresses the act of physical cohesive momentum.

The Spirit and Soul create from their unity their child, the Arch Angel **Uriel**, God is my light, the Angelic force of the physical world and from whom is breathed the force of physical life; the force **Sandalfon**. It is said in ancient manuscripts that this is the Arch Angelic force who 'gathers the prayers as he stands and they turn into flowers in his hands' This is the immense force of thought that communes with humanity's hopes, prayers and dreams. The higher intellect of humanity is bonded within this force of prayer.

The children of this Arch Angel have been given the name **Ishim**, the glorified souls. These are the aspects of humanity who have evolved to the highest potential on the Earth. They have risen in their Body of Glory and are forever part of the astral and etheric worlds that surround physical reality. The body of Glory is a separate emanation form the physical body and is created from the energy of the harmonisation of the all the other aspects of the human being. Each time a human overcomes an experience and communes with their own higher 'real' source, the source of the Creator, an energy is released that begins to form the body of Glory. When this is complete the human leaves this force behind and travels within and communes with the many dimensions of creation. The body of glory is forever part of the astral life of the Earth and can be reached by the prayers and love of humanity. The word Ishim in some countries is the word for gold. We can see the connection with this word and the accumulation of the quintessence of sunlight, seen by the ancients as the origins of precious gold found in the Earth.

The physical world; the speed of light has increased so much that the energy gathers together and 'particles', atoms, appear to be held together in their own 'spin', replicating the continual Birth of God. The force has gained such momentum, such speed, that it appears 'quantum'. It appears to be chaotic, but this is due to the imperceptibly fast oscillation, as creation becomes manifest. The physical universe is compelled to continually expand, the source of life is infinite and creation is infinitely unfolding within itself, constantly replicating the same fractal patterns of creation. This has been described as **Olahm Eretz**, all things within creation, the Earth and Universe, within the Creator. This is world named **Assiah**, that which has combined throughout many gravitations and experiences, to become manifest within the life force of the Creator.

# A Pause For Thought

The shattering of the vessels is a vital phase in the formulation of the Sephirot and the creation of the Tree of Life matrix of energies. Each Sephira becomes over full in its state of permanent reception. This bursting out of energy form each Sephira, is the first primal emissive possibility, recreating the process of the birth of primordial light. As each the primal Sephira shatters, the principle of giving out, of an eternal repetition of polarity, receptive and emissive states of being, are formed. Each and every phase is constant, perpetual and co exists. The primal lightening flash of pure light is the primal Tree of Life, each Sephira is in a constant state of shattering, reverberation and vibration, rebounding and receding into itself, stabilising and founding the perpetual matrix of light and sound vibrations.

The immense light forces that are released rebound against the light of Ain Soph Aur, forcing the process to retract, draw back and compound into a new stable structure.

The Sephirot emit energy, harnessing their own 'self' their own feeling, their own 'emotion' of recognition, this causes reverberation. Immeasurable light energy emits such force that it causes reverberation; reverberation or recognition. This formulates as 'sound'; Structure, 'pathways' establish themselves, linking each other with 'self recognition'; with sound.

# Human Communion with the Tree of Life

Each nucleus of light, the Sacred name of the living light Spirit, that observes and recognises itself within the reverberation sound and the formation of the Sephira, is the culmination of all that has taken place before. It is the living embodiment of the discoveries and experiences and recognitions that have led to that moment; each and every minutiae existing permanently, at the same time and forever.

The sacred name of the nucleus, the name of light, the name God, is an intense vibration of absolute light. The nucleus is the Spirit, the ever emitting force of perfect light. Humans are able to commune with this through their sense of sight. Our ability to draw in the light and heat of the sun, is a gateway to communing with the source of creation and the quintessence of the nucleus of each Sephira.

The more intense our awareness and focus on physical light becomes, the greater our experience of the life force of the creator. Any physical light can be utilised for this purpose and, of course, the most vital focus must be upon the Sun. Breathing in the energy from sunlight is a magic key to life. Sunlight has the power to transform everything from our emotions to our health. Never underestimate the life giving force of the Sun. If we truly want to understand the essence of the God and creation, then begin with communing with the intelligence and unending abundance of the light of the Sun.

The world of the Spirit can be described as the world of Division; a continual division of light, that divides continually from its own infinite source.

The human spirit, replicates this division of the life force within its own existence. The human spirit constantly divides, sending its energy throughout its different bodies and aspects until it physically dies and withdraws once more to the source from whence it came; only to begin again its constant division and experience of life in all dimensions and evolution. The spirit is the immense force of light and the quintessence of life. It cannot be damaged or tainted in any way. It is life. It is light. The spirit is the division of the 'one' the eternal; the infinite.

Each Sephira resonates in awareness and is the quintessence of sound energy. Each Sephira 'sings' its own recognition of existence. The Tree of Life is the embodiment of Divine harmony. The receptive waves of energy created by the Spirit nucleus of light are a reaction and logical consequence of the Spirit. This resonance is the receptive Soul, that 'feels' existence. The Soul or name of the Sephira vibrates in harmony with the 'feeling' of being. The Soul continually becomes the process of precession, an infinite eddying of 'feeling, vibrating and resonating the sound of creation. This description of 'feeling' is the perfect constant and ever abundant outpouring of unconditional 'feeling' and sensation. This is the source of 'emotion', in its purest and highest form. The essence of resonance, the source and perfection of harmony, that responds in perfect vibrational communion with the Spirit and force of life. Humans commune with the Sephirot with their sense of hearing. Their own sense of hearing is a communion with the world of harmony, with the universal and eternal soul. Music can lift us to the world of Divine resonance and harmony; we can feel our own souls vibrating in harmony with the Sephirot.

The Soul may be equated with multiplication; a continuum of infinite multiplication; of unbounded resonance. The soul flows unceasingly outward. The eddying of sound, of the perfect harmony of 'feeling'.

The human soul replicates this experience. It too constantly multiplies. The soul only gives outward. It emanates harmony that can be described as 'love'. This is the highest 'emotional' body, love only flows outward and cannot 'demand' or 'desire' the soul's only reality is vibrating is harmony with the spirit in ever flowing waves of 'giving'. A soul cannot be crushed, damaged or hurt in any way. It cannot be traded, compromised or sold. The soul is eternal and constant.

The Spirit and Soul, the Divine Father and the Divine Mother, create, by their union, the child of ether, the living being of perfect thought. The name of the Arch Angel emits perfume, the Divine fragrance of absolute thought. This perfume is far beyond our human understanding, but with our sense of smell we can commune with the existence of the Arch Angel. The name of the Arch Angel is formulated with the vibration of immense thought and is emitted by fragrance. The Arch Angels are infinite and eternal; thought is infinite and eternal. Humans may commune with these Divine thought forces with their sense of smell. As thought is eternal, a smell has the power of taking us back to the past instantly, as it evokes a long forgotten memory. The sacred names of the Arch Angels, that exist in the regions nearest to our own physical life, have been retained in many of the world's religions and spiritual connections. The same names reoccur throughout the world, even though the higher knowledge of higher forces and dimensions of the creator may have been neglected. The sacred names of God, made of light, have not been studied or retained in human consciousness, by many; being farther and more remote from our daily lives. The Holy names of the Sephirot have often replaced the vital practise of communing with the Sacred Names of God. It is easier for humans to remember and commune with the names of the Sephirot, as they vibrate with sound energy, than the Sacred Names of Absolute Light frequency. Easier again is the communion with the names of the Arch Angels, created by perfect thought and fragrance, as their life force is forever recorded in perpetual memory.

The dimension of the Arch Angels may also be described as multiplying. The existence of absolute thought is eternal and constantly unfolding; multiplying. One thought generating another, constantly reaching out further and deeper within the light and life force of creation and becomes the instigator of each new aspect of creation itself.

The human aspect, or body, of the Higher Intellect is an image of its source, the higher etheric planes of life. The higher intellect also multiplies. It too is constantly looking beyond itself and into the cosmos, into the 'solution' and into the world of creation. The human higher intellect communes with the higher dimensions of thought frequency and becomes the creator of its own reality. Gradually as it evolves, it becomes more and more adept, along its journey as a creator and gradually harmonises with the laws of perfect logic and eternal life.

The children of the Arch Angel, the condensation of thought may be equated to the lower thought body or lower etheric body of humanity. These angelic Hosts also emit the dimensions of lower emotion. These vibrate and inhabit the dimensions of existence closest to the physical manifestation of creation. Humans inhabit these worlds almost exclusively. Humans commune with the entities closest to the physical world and live a life of thought and emotion. At first humans live untamed and raw emotion, but gradually through their experiences, they become more selective and begin to take stock of the consequences of this way of life.

The realms of the angelic hosts may be described as subtracting and adding. The lower etheric planes of thought subtract and the lower planes of emotion add.

The human consciousness also responds in the same pattern. All conscious life lives its life immersed in these dimensions; within a world of adding and subtracting. Some may say that they 'believe' only in a physical world; this statement in itself is a complete rejection of this statement. A belief does not exist in the physical world; it exists exclusively in the dimension of thought. The human state is almost entirely an experience of thought and emotion; almost entirely an experience of adding something that makes us 'feel' either 'good' or 'bad', our emotional(or astral) body adding and when it is unable, our 'lower thoughts' subtract, saying 'that's not good', the message then rebounding in the emotional body that returns unhappy sensation and so the exchange continues. In other words, a human existence is ninety percent anything other than physical. We believe in our opinions, our rights, our hopes, our sorrows and our dreams. None of this is physical.

Even our assessment of our environment is based on our emotional response, which is then backed up by our thoughts. How do we know that the 'astral' world exists, this astral world of emotion? We know because we feel it. We can 'feel' and assess whether a place has a good or unwelcoming energy, whether we feel comfortable there or not. We detect very quickly the unsaid feelings of those around us and in our environment. Neither the Spirit nor the Soul can be damaged, but the astral body can feel hurt in myriad ways, sending the message to be assessed by the mental body of lower thought, which will soon subtract and assert the injustice that it perceives.

Our lives are constantly reverberating to the energies within which we are immersed. We are in a constant state of ricochet; between the astral, emotional body and the lower thought body, adding and subtracting. These are our detection mechanisms, our barometer of how we are gravitating either farther away or close to our source, our divine and 'real' self, who dwells forever within and forever without, in the essence of Sephira Tifaret and can be embraced within the rays of the Sun.

The sense of taste connects us to the both the astral, emotional world and to the lower etheric world of thought. When we are emotionally upset we tend to eat, as this body adds up. When we are locked in the lower thought body, we do not eat, as this body subtracts.

When something does not feel 'right' or 'good' by simply asking the question 'am I adding' or 'am I subtracting' we have immediately lifted ourselves to the higher dimensions of the Higher Intellect and we will begin to search the world of solutions. If we commune with the sun and breathe in and guard the sunlight internally, cherishing each breath, we will fuse once more with our Christ essence, our higher or 'real' self. We can call on the infinite beings, the angelic hosts who inhabit the regions closest to the physical world and they will crowd round and give freely of their energy and begin their role of cleansing and uplifting and gathering our prayers.

The physical dimension is recognised by the sense of touch and also adds continually. The physical world adds and expands and manifests an eternal physical reality. The human experience has mimicked this 'adding' and expansion in curious ways, an endless creation of 'things' and an endless 'expansion' of economy; a material world. We wish to touch our creations; we wish to evaluate our success with all that we can touch. As humans evolve, as they begin to grow up, as a species, as we gravitate ever closer to our 'real' and best version of ourselves, a natural realisation occurs. This is realisation that there is an abundance of regenerating resources, more than enough to support us. That dividing is the natural process of the creation and of the Spirit; multiplying, is the role of the soul. Looking for solutions is the natural state of the higher aspect of thought. All these things are the origins of creation and humanity is bound inextricably and forever to replicate this process. The first primal Tree of Life is the expression of discovery, observation and verification. The vast mutable forces, the immeasurable vortices of light, the following precession as each Sephira and ensuing formations, are created by the 'lightening flash' of untamed force. This state of creation and shattering is perpetual; eternal.

There is no distinction or time; the following phase of logic, of harmonisation and stability is a cause of and eternally bound within the primal tree. One is not opposed to the other, but one tree, each within itself, a coexistence, an embodiment of poetic logic; a holographic infinity.

The Tree becomes stable by the vibration of energy drawing back; reverberating. The energy cannot diffuse, as there are no limits within the light of Ayn Sof Aur. The energy must constantly gather momentum and constantly create more vortices and pinpoints of absolute light nuclei.

As the Tree becomes more stable, pathways of light compound the tree between the Sephira, static geometrical energy begins its discovery and will eventually lead to the principle of physical manifestation. Each pathway is a result of light, creating sound vibration, that has become continually more formed, more precisely 'tuned'.

Each and every phase of creation is a step of absolute logic, one phase following and flowing from the direct logical cause.

Each phase and verification coexists eternally and all in perpetuity.

| Higher Nature | | | | | |
|---|---|---|---|---|---|
| Sephirotic Gateway | Sephirotic Name of God | | | | |
| The Spirit | The world of the spirit. The World of light | The element of fire | The sense of sight | The capacity to divide | First triad of the Sephirotic Tree of Atziluth corresponding to Yad |
| The Soul | The world of the Soul the world of sound | The element of water | The sense of hearing | The capacity to multiply | Second triad of the Sephirotic Tree of Beriyah corresponding to Yad Hé |
| The Higher intellect | The world of higher etheric thought the world of perfume. | The element of air | The sense of smell | The capacity to multiply | Third triad of the Sepohirotic Tree corresponding to Yetzrah. Yad HéVav |

| Lower Nature | | | | | |
|---|---|---|---|---|---|
| The Lower mental body | The world of lower thoughts. The etheric planes | The element of air | The sense of taste | The capacity to subtract | |
| The Astral body | The world of lower emotions. The astral planes | The lower element of water | The sense of taste | The capacity to add | |
| The will to survive. physical body | The physical world | The element of earth | The sense of touch | The capacity to add | Fourth triad of the Sephirotic tree Assiah corresponding to Yad Hé Vav Hé |

# A Pause For Thought

The poetic, elegant unfolding of numbers, the one, travelling forward, becoming two, the turning and reconnecting, the twisting and moving of becoming each news phase of creation, is at every moment of arrival, a new and unique Birth of God. The immense, dynamic force of creation, that is suspended in an eternal state of formation of the Sephirot, is the energy of light itself; light so far beyond our human comprehension, that only a small essence of this divine light can be gleaned from a human being contemplating the sun. The speed and force of momentum, gathers itself into a centrifugal point of light and then the beautiful about turn, twist of the light energy, creates the transition of force, creating the dimensions beneath, that will become more and more dense and will finally manifest as the seemingly physical world; illustrated by the 'DNA' twist of numbers, which visible nature will later repeat endlessly. All of this is in a continual waterfall of overflowing, and drawing back into itself and stabilising another endless possibility of creation. The next journey of sound itself, the journey of the creation of each precise sound, is depicted by each Holy letter of the creative process. The stability of the Sephirotic tree suspended and stabilised in eternal sound vibration, revolves in perpetual harmony.

This continual process of discovery, observation, resonance in recognition (which we can equate with emotion) is the also human experience. Humanity created in the image of God. This image of experience, that everything is verified as a reality by our emotional recognition and thus, further compounded by our working upon this emotional recognition with thought; the ultimate discoverer, observer and verifier.

The human being is the ultimate journey of becoming the creator. The human creation and evolution is the ultimate pinnacle of the perpetual Birth of God.

# FURTHERMORE

We can see this process illustrated in the symbolism of the Tarot. The wands or fire representing the Yad, the firey force of the spirit, which is mutable and dynamic. The Father force.

The cups represent the water, the soul. The fluid resonance of sound and acceptance, are created by precession from the nucleus of the spirit (illustrated as the wand). The feminine receptive Hé; mutable and dynamic, resonating its recognition of the ignition of the spirit.

The swords, the child, the force of air, 'thought'. This is the holy letter Vav. Stabilised and directed, building the stability of the Tree of Creation and Life itself. Formulating the static geometry that will further manifest into physical creation.

The disks, the earth, the compounded, feminine daughter; Isis unveiled or visible nature. The physical world made of stable, static geometrical energy. This is the holy letter Hé in its manifest form.

We can see the further compounding of each element in the procession of the court cards.

From a human perspective we can easily feel the process of the Spirit, the Shin, Divine fire or imagination. The receptive soul, accepting and 'feeling' it to be good.

The further direction of thought, swiftly followed by the second watery emotional response and verification.

If enough energy 'attention' is given to the emotion then it continues to compound, finally manifesting into a physical experience. Drawn into existence by the laws of 'magnetism' or attraction, gathering together to manifest, or compound, around the swiftly gathering momentum of the thought and emotion.

**The Holy Letters**

Each letter is a force of the creative process, a numerical power, which breathes life and formulates every phase of manifestation. There is a wealth of literature over thousands of years devoted to the deepest understanding of the sacred letters. One lifetime is not enough to uncover the secret depths of profound wisdom that each letter expresses.

There are three emanations of letters, the three Maternal letters, or primary forces that are mothers or gateways to the dimensions of creation and flow across the Sephirotic Tree.

The seven planetary letters; forces that harness and generate the energy, that will focus light energy toward manifestation.

The twelve zodiacal letters that formulate the phases of the creative process that will become the experience of the physical world. These flow, create stability, and a framework for physical life to unfold.

Together these become the twenty two forces of sound frequency that 'sing' life into being. This illustrates the entire process of achievement, polarity that has accomplished stability and become the dwelling place of the life force of the creator, in the heavens and upon the earth.

The creator draws from within the forces and energies that are a permanent and pre-existing part of the first solid structure, the first complete template of the creative process. The letters are predestined to be written, according to their forces of energy upon the story of all that may be created.

There is only one letter and one number; the Holy letter Yad, the symbol of the hand of God. This is the numerical power of the ten; the one and the zero, the spirit and physical matter, represented by the one, from whence all else flows, the magician's wand and the entire Sephirotic Tree. It is combined with the zero, the space within which physical matter will reside.

This tiny letter begins its journey of momentum, twisting and turning, reaching forward and beyond, creating and compounding self discovery into separate experiences and realities. All the sacred letters are made from the holy Yad.

Each letter and sound draws its essence from the epicentre of sound and energy that is the Yad. The focus of sound is a metathesis, the quintessence of sound in a focussed journey into letters and words.

## The First Letter **Aleph**

The letter is created by two 'yadim' and a division between them. This illustrates the Divine World above and the Physical world below. It shows us the fluid separation between them, the separation between the waters and the waters.

This represents humanity, receiving with one hand from the heavens and channelling the energies into the physical world. This can be equated to the dance of the Whirling Dervish, who is the living Aleph, spinning in space, in Hebrew our Echad; our minute but vital place of being, spinning within the vastness of the cosmos.

The Aleph expresses the breath of life. Aleph has been given the symbol of the Ox, the raw force of nature.

The living sacred Aleph, the number one, is soundless and the instant before speech. Begin to say the word Aleph and stop just before you make the sound. This is Aleph.

## The **Beth**

Creation begins with the sacred letter Beth. The holy Beth is the numerical power of two, the glyph which is a human, kneeling at prayer. Beth was chosen as the first letter of the creative process and the first letter of Baruch, to bless, so that all that flowed from creation would be blessed.

The Beth has been given the symbol of the House. A dwelling place for all that is blessed. The Beth creates the first formulated sound, 'b'; the first sound that a baby makes when attempting to speak cognitive words.

Beth also creates the sound 'v', a secondary wave that carries the blessings of the creator through the middle of a word and onwards into the cosmos.

The Beth breathes life into the physical force of all which will later formulate the planet mercury. The symbol of the planet mercury illustrates the initiate, who has devoted his being to combining the emissive masculine forces of the sun and the receptive feminine forces of the moon, in harmony with the earth.

## The **Gimel**

The holy Gimel has become the numerical force of three. It is the first letter of the word 'gomel', to give. The gimel is the sound 'g'. This letter has been given the symbol of the camel. The beast of burden who survives in harsh conditions, where there is little water. Water represents the emotional body, which continually has the need to add to itself. The camel has its own internal resources that carry him long distances and is of service to others. The words 'it is easier for a camel to pass through the eye of a needle than for a rich man to reach heaven' may be understood by beginning to contemplate the holy Gimel. The 'eye' of the needle' is the narrow entrance to the upper most regions of the Sephirotic Tree, from whence the holy Gimel flows. Someone 'rich', with their emotional needs cannot reach these heights. Only someone who has calmed and tamed their lower nature, their lower emotional body, is 'poor' enough to pass through this pathway to experience the diving heavenly regions of peace.

The force of the holy Gimel formulates the physical moons. The earth's moon expresses the 'poverty' of having no light of its own, but is able to receive and share the light of the sun and lights the night sky for travellers in the dark. The water and tides of the earth, even the cycles of women are influenced by the moon. In this way the holy Gimel teaches how to tame the insatiable demands of the lower emotional body in order to receive the divine light and share it amongst others. The Gimel is the bountiful and continual sharing of the eternal light of the creator.

## The **Dalet**

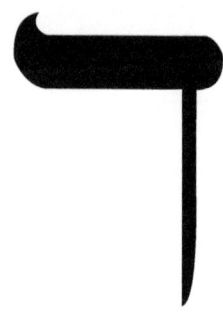

The holy Dalet is forever in communion with the Gimel. The Dalet is the numerical force of four and the formulates the sound 'd'. It has been given the symbol of the doorway. Dalet is the doorway to highest and most sacred regions of the Sephirotic Tree .This letter express that there is only the one force of the creator, that there is nothing other than this; it expresses 'selflessness', 'having no light of her own'. The Gimel bestows the light of the creator to the Dalet, who is 'poor' or empty. The symbolism of the doorway expresses this; a door may open to something, but has no other purpose. The Dalet is the gateway to the Beth, the house, the dwelling place of God.

The physical reality of the planet Venus is formulated by the Dalet. Venus is said to be the 'feminine' receptive force and the planet created by divine love. The truth of profound, unconditional love can only flow outwardly, it has no experience of 'self'.

## The **Hé**

The holy letter Hé was originally drawn as a man with his hands stretched upwards, as though beholding a wondrous sight. The Hé is the numerical power of five, the receptor of the spirit of the creator. The sound of Hé is 'h' in the back of the throat. The Hé has been given the symbol of the 'window' through which divine light shines. Hé is the first of the zodiacal forces that begin the process of physical creation, Aries. The Hé can be heard in the sound of the early morning in spring time. The Hé can be seen in the dawn and the rising sun. The Hé can be felt in morning dew and the trickling of the first streams after the winter snows have thawed.

When the silver light glints on the seas and lakes, we can begin to feel the Hé. The Hé is the Arien force of the leaf buds bursting out in spring.

## The **Vav**

The holy letter Vav is the numerical force of six. The six is the key to the creation of the all. The sound of Vav is 'v'. It is also a vowel sound 'ow' and 'uw'. This letter is drawn as a 'hook' and is sometimes described as a 'nail', the Vav is the force that connects the heavens and the earth and is the sign of the messiah; one who connects the divine worlds to the earthly plane. The Vav is the sign of the great Initiates and the zodiacal force of Taurus. This is the symbolism of 'Jesus' being 'nailed' to the cross; the cross of the initiates, the Tree of Life itself.

Taurus is the time of the warm earth, stable and full of all the components that are ready to begin their cycle of birth and abundance.

## The **Zayn**

The holy Zayn is the numerical power of seven. The Zayn expresses the seventh phase of creation, of 'rest' or 'recognition' of the accomplishment of the creative process. The sound of Zayn is 'z'. The Zayn emits the zodiacal force of Gemini, the communicative and expressive force that travels within the power of thought. The symbol given to Zayn is the sword or weapon. This represents the sword of perfected thought. Thought that is directed, honed and tuned in order to convey its message. The messiah 'comes with a sword', this is the Zayn, the messenger and conveyor of perfected thought frequency.

## The **Chet**

The holy Chet is the numerical power of eight. This figure, eight, shows us the flowing of energies from the divine world above to the formulated world beneath. The sound of Chet is 'kh'. The Chet expresses 'hovering' as an eagle hovers above the nest in order to feed her young. This is the 'Chet' the spirit of the creator hovering above the face of the deep; the separator of quintessence. This is illustrated by the symbol given to it, that of an enclosure or fence.

The Chet is the force of Cancer. The shell of the crab expresses this force of separating. The Chet is the building phase of creation.


## The **Tet**

The holy Tet is the number force of nine; the ultimate culmination of all the numbers. The sound of Tet is 't'. This is the heat of the spirit that heats up all the components and sends them irradiating in space. The symbol of Tet is the serpent of divine wisdom and the intensity of the fire of the creative spirit.

The Tet is the force of Leo and the letter can be seen as representing a lion with his tail curled over his back. The force of Leo is the immeasurable power of the igniting spirit into the whole of creation.

## The **Yad**

The holy Yad, the essence from whence all the other letters are drawn. The number force of ten, the spirit and the physical dimensions. The sound of Yad is 'y'.

The symbol of the hand, shows us that all has been accomplished by the creator; all is life resides within the hand of the creator.

The Yad is the power of Virgo and the physical realms that have their potential within the hand of God.

This is the sixth zodiacal phase of potential and of physical culmination. The Yad is small, like a grain of seed that holds within it the secret of the tree and the creation of forests. From this one small seed a universe is born.

## The **Kaf**

The holy Kaf is the numerical power of twenty. The sound of Kaf is 'K' and 'kh'. Kaf is drawn in two ways, bent over and straight. The bent Kaf illustrates the children of light who bend to and accept the power of the creator. The two aspects of Kaf are desire and joy; the desire of knowing the exhilaration of communion with the creator and the overwhelming joy that this bestows. The Kaf describes the freedom of bending to the power of life and the creator. The second straight Kaf illustrates the creator reaching down to his children. It describes one person including another. The Kaf unfolds and reaches down to become the second illustration of 'inclusion'. The symbol of Kaf is the palm of the hand. The Kaf is the first letter of Kether, the crown, the glory of the creator. The Kaf is the eleventh letter and also the eleventh letter of the western alphabet. The numerical force of eleven shows the pure spirit that is infinite and has ignited life in all dimensions of creation. It is eternally self realising, self generating and self fulfilling. The K being the eleventh letter of the western alphabet is why it is the first letter of Kabbalah, when written phonetically. This is the key of infinity and eternity. The Kaf is perpetuity.

### The **Lamed**

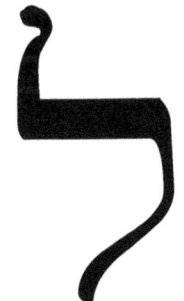

The holy Lamed is the numerical force of thirty and forms the sound 'l'. The lamed breathes the zodiacal phase of Libra, the time of balance and equilibrium. The perfection of the seventh day of creation, the seventh zodiacal phase, the pause, the suspension after the creative process has been accomplished. This is the sublime moment of light shining through a prism and creating the seven colours of visible light. The Lamed is the only letter that stretches up above the line when written. Its symbol is the staff of the herdsman. The word Lamed, may pronounced also as Lamad, to teach and Lamud, disciple. The staff of Moses symbolised his role as guide and teacher, also that of a disciple of the creator.

### The **Mem**

The holy Mem is the numerical force of forty and forms the sound 'm'. The symbol of the Mem is water. There are two ways of writing Mem, the first when in the middle of a word and the second when appearing at the end of a word .The first resembles a wave, that flows and the second is circular. This explains that the wave flows out and draws back; it conveys rhythm and motion, the sea washing up against the shore. The second shows the circular progress of water. That water is always part of the whole, each drop belongs to the source and will take part in an eternal cycle of visiting the earth and rejoining the source. This represents the soul and its union with the one eternal soul. Mem represents the

Torah, its wisdom flowing to humanity and the closed Mem protecting its secrets within.

## The **Nun**

The holy Nun is the numerical force of fifty and creates the sound 'n'. The symbol of Nun is the fish. The fish represents the human soul swimming in the oceans of the Mem. This formulates the zodiacal force of Scorpio. This is immense culmination of the forces of nature that will harness and shape the physical world. The Nun expresses the process and life, death and reincarnation. The cycle of the souls. The fish swims in a hidden sea, within the vast oceans of Mem, the waters of the universal soul. The Nun tells us that those who see only the physical world are deceiving themselves.

## The **Samekh**

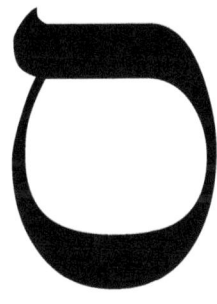

The holy Samekh is the numerical force of sixty and forms the sound 's'. The Samekh is the force which formulates the zodiacal phase of Sagittarius. The symbolism of the Sagittarian centaur, illustrates the harnessing of the physical and the higher dimension, to work in unity, shooting the arrow of intention back again into the divine regions. The Samekh is described 'to support'. This is the meaning of the symbol of the prop, given to this letter. It follows the Nun, supporting those who are unable to see the divine in their lives and reality of the dimensions of existence beyond. The letter is circular, depicting the eternal cycles of life.

The **Ayn**

The holy Ayn is the numerical power of seventy and its symbol is the eye. The Ayn has no sound of its own. It is empty and only resonates with the sound of the vowel placed within it. This is the force of Capricorn, the force of crystallisation, of solidifying; the only choice is to give in to decay and decomposition when the life force becomes too suppressed and constricted. It is released through decay. All that is obsolete is absorbed by the earth and used to generate life once more. All is overseen by the 'eye' of the creator. The Ayn expresses both to see and to be seen. The eye represents the spirit; always active, always present, always observant. The figure is drawn with two eyes, and are

described as the 'five kindnesses' and the 'five mights'. These are the hidden energies of Sephira Da ath, knowledge.

## The **Pe**

The holy Pe has the numerical force of eighty and the symbol given to it is the mouth. The Pe creates the sound P or F. This is force that formulates the planetary energy of Mars. This is the heat of the furnace, the energy of fire and molten lava, that heats up the over solidified matter of the phase of Capricorn. The perpetual force of the spirit works upon stagnated matter, igniting its own essence once more. From the mouth, the wisdom seen and recognised by Ayn is transmitted. This is the knowing of knowledge. The power of Daath is concealed in the mouth. Pe expresses the voice of God through the mouth.

## The **Tzaddi**

The holy Tzaddi is the numerical force of ninety and symbol of Tzaddi is the fish hook. The symbol of the fisherman goes far back in history to the symbol of the Ibis, the fisher who stands in the ancient rivers, balancing on one leg with a bent knee. He fishes in the ancient wisdom in the sacred river of life. The Ibis was the symbol for secret wisdom. This can be seen in Masonic rituals today and many esoteric statues. Tzaddi is connected to the back of the head. This is where the subtle entrances, where divine entities draw close, are concealed. The Tzaddi is the zodiacal force of Aquarius. The symbol of the water carrier represents the human being, the bridge between the heavens and the earth, collecting the sacred waters of the life force and pouring them onto the earth. This illustrates the divine river of life, flowing once more into the physical planes, from on high. The Tzadi resembles the Alpeh and is the communion with the first holy letter. The symbol of Aquarius also depicts the Aleph. The Tzadi is the master of the Universe, one who draws from the heavens and blessings the earth with divine quintessence. This is humanity, created in the image of God.

### The **Qoph**

The sacred Qoph formulates the numerical power of one hundred and has been given the symbol of the eye of a needle and also the ear. This reminds us of the state of awareness, of intense listening to the voice of the creator, that allows us to become our 'echad' our fulfilling of divine creation, fusing with the creator on every level of existence. The letter is drawn with a resh and a descending Zayn, transmitting the divine from the higher dimensions. The Qoph conceals the secret of the unutterable holiness of the creator. The Qoph is also shown as a 'monkey', resembling a man, but an animal. It describes the human quest to rise up and touch the spiritual heights in themselves. The eye of the needle reminds us of the narrow opening into to mysteries of the creator, hidden within the most remote regions of the Sephirotic Tree.

This is the zodiacal phase of Pisces. The symbol of the two fish, illustrate the soul flowing backwards and forwards, throughout many incarnations, within the universal soul.

This is the phase when the divine river of life recedes and is drawn back once more into its source.

The Qoph describes the cycles of eternity. This is observed within the cycles of the moon and is recorded as the cycles of the Jewish calendar. The Qoph reveals the feminine force of the moon and the cycles of life and death.

## The **Resh**

The holy Resh is the numerical force of two hundred and has been given the symbol of the head. The Resh is the former of the suns. The force of sun is the ancient secret.

The essence of the sun is the life force itself and the physical representation of the light of the creator. To touch upon the immensity of light, study the physical light of the sun. The story of creation is found in the rays of the sun.

The Resh shows constant transition, the life force reaching even the depths of the earth, warming and blessing the earth into growth and abundance. The Resh is a leader and a life giver. Resh is the central letter of the word Bereshit, the central letter of the process of creation and the flourishing of the physical world.

## The **Shin**

The holy Shin forms the numerical force of three hundred and has been given the symbol of the tooth. The Shin is the element of divine fire. It is drawn with three teeth, that resemble flames. The Shin ignites and consumes, the teeth represent eating and consuming of energies. The three pillars of the Shin are the three columns of the Tree of Life. They appear flaming with divine quintessence. The whole cycle of transformation healing, breaking and restoring is described in the formation of the letter. The Shin portrays the constant and unwavering divine light that transcends all aspects of life.

The three pillars, formed by three Vavs show the balance of all aspects of life, the discipline of following the middle pillar which is the stability of creation.

The Shin is the principle of light, the essence of all creation.

## The **Tav**

The holy Tav is the culmination of the number forces in the power of four hundred. The symbol of the Tav is the cross. The physical world is formed around the cross. The Tav is a seal or a divine sign. It is sealed on all humanity who is destined to become one with the creator and is to perfect the art of creation.

Tav is the last letter and the last letter of Bereshit. This describes that the end was there at the beginning and there is no end to creation. 'I am Aleph and Tav, the first and the last. That which 'is, was and will be' This expresses that all things are permanent, 'now' and infinite. This illustrates that every aspect and phase of creation is perpetual and co existing.

# A Pause for Thought

How does this knowledge affect humanity? Why does it matter? Why is the knowledge of the Hebrew letters so important; does this mean that Hebrew is better than any other language? Is there a divine language? Is there a common language?

These are the questions that naturally occur.

Language is an intentional harnessing of sound vibration in order to convey a particular frequency.

Firstly it is important to contemplate that the formation of the Sephirotic Tree, and of every dimension of creation is a journey of absolute logic; every phase causing the natural and logical phase, a perfect result of the energy from whence it was born. The first impetus is movement, the second, observation and the third recognition. This can be seen as a simple equation

$$\text{NOTHING} + \text{MOVEMENT} = \text{IGNITION} = \text{LIGHT} = \text{OBSERVATION} = \text{RECOGNITION}$$

This 'recognition' releases waves or energy, or sound. The first essential state of the creative progression and of all creation is absolute logic; cause and effect. Each 'awareness', or Sephira, of the creator is a natural answer, result and resonance of all that has come before. No plan, no desire, or wanting, or intention, exists. The progress of logic is the creative force. Logic is the life force itself. Logic is the evolutionary journey in every dimension and every aspect of life.

The evolutionary discovery of existence is the discovery into consciousness. The instant of 'Ehieh' 'I am' and at the same time conveying 'I will be' predicts the arrival at intention. The progression of creation, of coming into being as every name of God is born and each Sephira resounds with recognition, becomes a more verified experience and gravitates nearer toward intention.

Logic precedes intention. The moment of intention is a result of consciousness and focussed being. Intention itself is the result of logic. The energy which created the first immense expression of speed created the first vortex of light, the spinning vortex created the first focus, caused by immeasurable momentum. This first point of absolute being is the epicentre of focus.

The moment of focus produces the result of energy waves of recognition or resonance; or sound. The natural progress from the two polarities of focus and recognition is the harnessing of both energies to produce a result; this evolves to be focussed intention. Therefore language is the result of this progression.

The moment of intention is a natural and unwavering progression of energy, followed by the harnessing of sound into intention; an intention of formulating sound and focussing the momentum of the creative force into the next logical phase. The harnessing of the power of sound as particular letters, with itemised sounds is in the divine sense, language.

The potential for every itemised sound pre exists within the original template of structure, from whence all creation repeats its patterns of form. Each 'power' point express a life force that becomes a unique sound vibration. This is the divine language. The Hebrew letters, that have close a correspondence to other ancient languages, replicate these original currents of sound, that traverse the simple, original template of creation.

This illustrates the importance of sound itself, it is the force of creation in the physical world, inspired and instigated by light. From a human perspective, it also illustrates the importance of using words carefully, particularly as words are preceded by thought and clothed with emotion, adding energy on many planes, before the sound wave is released into the world; already away on its journey, formulated by precise intention.

The entire formation of the Sephirotic Tree is shaped by logic, the existence of each potential and possibility, entirely as a result of its own 'non existence'. 'Nothing' cannot 'be', without its recognition of nothingness. This instantly creates its own simultaneous potential of 'being'; of something and of all potential creation. This instantly brings about two states, two polarities; receptive and emissive, 'feminine' and 'masculine'. These two co existing states and their differences together create movement, thus propelling the entire voyage of infinite creation.

The initial momentum and speed created by the first process of implosion, causes a velocity of whirling movement, resulting in the first pin point or what appears to be, the first nucleus of absolute light. The reverberations and waves of this impact are the primal 'recognition' of 'being' or the primal birth of God. The Creator's journey of self discovery is one of perfect logic, followed by recognition. The arrival of each coming into being, by velocity and momentum, results in each light nucleus, followed by self recognition. The process of stability, or the appearance of stability, from the human perspective, is formed by this recognition, this secondary wave of energy created by the pin point of light within the ocean of light. This secondary result is the primal wave of sound. From the perspective of the creator, it is a journey of developing recognition; a journey of sublime light and harmony, an infinite and incomparable voyage of perpetual unfolding, infinite arrival and constant awakening of revelation and recognition.

The velocity of the initial implosion and the continual, co existing, timeless and infinite states of the birth of God, compel the never ending momentum of creation. The Sephirotic Tree is in a constant state of motion; repeating the light vortex, the ever self perpetrating and infinite creation of Sephirot. The formation of individual 'letters' are formed by the vortex spins and graceful 'DNA' twists of all that is dictated by the flourishing of numbers and moments of their coming into reality.

All potential exists within the first stable dimension of Bereshit; within the Blessed Six.

The graceful movement of the spinning and twisting energies of creation begin to trace patterns within the primal stability. Each movement, gathering energy of self recognition and the realisation of shapes begin to appear. These are the creator's first experience of metathesis. This is the divine language of harnessed light.

All of these stages, momentums and harnessing of energies are constant and co existing, eternally.

These are all eternal, dwelling within the continual birth of God. The process of creation is the continual, developing awareness of the creator. The step by step logical progression of cause and effect brings the Sephirotic Tree of Life into reality. God is a perpetual evolution. The mind of God is a gradual development; a voyage of discovery and recognition. Every minute resonance of life, whether it be the life force of a blade of grass growing, the heartbeat of each species on the planet or the grand creation of galaxies in the cosmos, is the evolution and experience of God.

The process of creation is the result of movement. Time is movement. Each Birth of God, of coming into being, each 'name' of a Sephira, is a result of momentum. Because all is within, all is implosion within infinity.

Momentum gathers and is replayed; as continual and graceful vortices of energy. The elegant spin of the Sephirotic Tree itself becomes the illusion of time. Time is a turning ellipse of energy that as it turns, greets itself in close encounters. This is why we can sometimes see into past or future windows of time, as the space between times is only a breath between. Time only appears to exist from one small perspective and one small instant in the infinite turning of movement and energy.

# Telesma

In the beginning was the word

The accumulation of energy that gathers through the process of graceful movement, gathers together at each twist and turn to present letters. The first metathesis, the transition of letter forms into language, into a vibrating word, is constantly present in the structure of creation. This word is Telesma. It contains the end and the beginning, the Tav and the Aleph. It is created by the momentum of the three Mother letters. These three letters create the gateways of each accumulating light frequency. They give birth to each dimension of more dense and more manifest light energy. The perpetual result of light frequency is its recognition in sound and harmony. The three letters, propelled by divine fire sing creation into reality. Telesma is light and 'let there be light'. This is the vibration of creation and the resonance of the cosmos. Telesma is the force of life.

God was, is, and will be, eternally nothing and everything, eternally silent and The Word. The word is gathered by momentum, cause and effect and is compelled by a perpetual unfolding of logic.

From a human perspective, the only way to attempt to describe the wondrous feeling of the birth of each moment of creation is 'feel'. Our own human emotions, our experience of love, of joy, of bliss are very pale reverberations of the vast explosions of conscious self recognition of the creator. These 'feelings' are a tiny drop in the ocean of immensity. Imagine that you are standing on top of a mountain and looking out at the most wonderful view, or looking up at myriad stars in a perfect night sky. Imagine this if you are in love and equally loved in return. This exaltation is a minute reverberation of the 'feeling' of the creator, the reality of God.

The stunning sounds of a human choir, re-creating the harmonies that we describe as angelic, is a fragment of the divine harmony in an eternal euphoria of creation. This is the voice, the language of the spheres and the song of God.

The ancient Hebrew letters were received by the great sages and given as a gift to humanity. This was the gift of harmonising with the creator. These divine letters, formed by divine physics are the key to reverberating in unity and harmony with every aspect of God and every instant of creation.

Humanity is not so much waking up, as growing up

*Shema Israel YHVH Elohaynu YHVH echad*

Listen, Oh child of light, to the voice of the creator within you. The one God within whom all things dwell, who is the one and has become many, but remains the one. Shine in your unique and vital part of the one, in the infinite vastness of creation.

"The sins of the Fathers are visited upon the descendants unto the second generation."

This ancient phrase sums up the effect, not only genetically but emotionally and mentally, of the problems caused by our ignorance of the laws of cause and effect. The natural 'growing up' of a human being manifests as "a taking of responsibility" not only for their emotions and thoughts, but for the effects of those generations who have come before. A child carries the emotional results of the parents. This behaviour, which can often be severely detrimental, is often passed on and replayed for several generations. A pattern may take at least three generations before an individual, the product of this, has evolved into an incarnation where they are adult enough to not only be aware of the damage that has been inherited but also responsible enough to take on the task of laying aside the victim role and deciding to take control of the health and happiness of future generations. It is said that a wise man plants a tree that will bear fruit long after his death.

A child who has been subjected to abuse feels guilty or responsible for their experiences. No amount of rational thinking or counselling will annihilate these feelings. This is because there is, in subtle way an exchange of energies that have been, in many instances, deliberately created by the perpetrator. This is a general illustration of how energies attract experience. Each individual experience is unique. There are many and diverse aspects in every story to uncover. It is important to understand that the following example is not in way about 'blaming' the victim and is intended as a basic example of how patterns create energies in the subtle bodies that intertwine with those of a perpetrator. An example of this exchange of energies is that of a child who is particularly vulnerable. A child who has not been made to feel particularly worthy has in their energy an emotional need to be made to feel special. A sexual groomer will find this child an easy subject and will gradually build up a relationship whereby the child starts to feel special. This then escalates into physical abuse. The child is easily manipulated because they sense a complicity in the events. They sense that they have somehow drawn this to them. This manifests as a deep seated belief in their guilt. Without a deeper understanding of the accumulated emotional escrow in their emotional reality, it is very hard to truly eliminate this guilt. It is equally very difficult for the child to go through adult life without attracting further abuse because of the need to be seen as worthy. The energy of the past continues to vibrate in the astral or lower emotional body of each person. Sometimes it takes several generations to disperse.

This escalates into huge energies, accumulated from the past. This manifests often as war on national and international scales. An absurd mentality has grown up within humanity. A juvenile grooming of the young to enter an army with the idea of becoming special, a hero, is not intelligent. Creating armies is grooming the unsuspecting.

The world is currently controlled by fear. Fear of our neighbours, fear of other cultures, fear of the food we eat, the air we breathe and even the sun that brings us life.

There is no shortage in the world. The world is abundant, magnificent, self sustaining and more than enough for all.

The playground games of media and politics will naturally be exposed and seen for what they are. The sudden arrival of the world of social media has very quickly begun to control many people. This is firstly due to the air based polarity of the age in which we live. The world of all air borne traffic, that busily and frantically controls the very perceived existence of the world's inhabitants. Many people gravitate toward mental instability and illness due to their fictitious lives carried out in the bizarre public platform of social media. A dependency upon continually posting and exposing their lives on this public platform often becomes dependency on thousands of people, completely unknown to them, 'liking' their posts. This is the first time in the history of the human race that people value themselves because of the gathering of 'friends' and the approbation of people who they will never know. Many people post pictures and accounts of their 'fabulous' and 'fun' lives that bear little or no resemblance to lives they really live; suffering in silence in a sense of unworthiness because their life does not stack up to everyone else's lives that are bandied about on social media.

This new phenomena is already waning and many are realising the negative impact of this on their real lives. This is world of virtual 'stardom' is only a banal example of the juvenile state of humanity that is coming to an end.

New generations will no longer take part in these playground games.

This will leave humanity free to use our wondrous technology to create a world of sanity, intelligence and peace.

Banking systems, poverty, wealth, lack, insurance against something that is unlikely to happen (we can see that the likelihood of disaster is so small that businesses make huge profits in creating insurance policies against the odds of these events) business based on fear has very shaky foundations.

Fictitious agendas show a lack of intelligence. Conspiracy theories that promote fear in every dark corner are not intelligent.

It is inane, childish and doomed to failure.

None of this is real or important.

The process of growing up has becoming highlighted. Under the spotlight and out of the creeping shadows come world leaders of spectacular childishness. For all the world see. Exposed, and soon to become obsolete.

Whilst attention is focussed on the big bad scary world, we become less and less in communion with that perfect version of ourselves, the 'real' integral vibrant, infinite you.

The only reality is life and the only purpose is creation.

Humanity is in a continual process of growing up. This process is speeding up magnificently.

One world, one nation, made of essential unique individuals.

By becoming as close as possible to the most perfect version of yourself, by speaking to and understanding that 'real' you, is the only way that humanity will create an intelligent world.

Becoming a responsible adult, by caring for and cleaning up our feelings, we will find that our thoughts will very quickly come into line. Humanity will evolve into a universal consciousness of intelligence, sharing the immense resources and abundance of the Earth, and using our immense resources of intelligence to care for the living planet and the living universe.

This is the evolution of the human race. This is the destiny of the physical journey of humanity.

Live your Kabbalah, that which is received in light by the shining ones and spoken through tradition, to the generations.

Each has their own Kabbalah, their experience and revelations. The teacher and the student are one, adding their own experiences to the whole vast accumulation of wisdom throughout the ages.

Live your own unique, perfect Kabbalah.

The soul of mankind is a blank page, always ready for a new song to be inscribed.

The natural state of humanity is hope. The natural and irreversible journey is evolution. Evolution is the development of intelligence. Intelligence on every level dictates. It is intelligent to create a world of harmony. It is intelligent to share.

The human race is beginning to understand and work with the laws of creation consciously. We are learning the exhilaration and fun of learning to manifest at will.

The realisation that we are all responsible for our own lives and for all that we create, based on our decisions to manage our feelings and thoughts, has already risen into the consciousness of many.

This is only the beginning.

These are the first faltering steps of humanity creating universes and dimension at will in the image of the creator.

True manifestation is the fusion with the

divine, fusion with the most perfect version of ourselves that we can imagine.

True manifestation is not about creating material luxuries and wealth, fun and good practise though that may be. True manifestation is far more exhilarating. True manifestation is an unbreakable communion with the Divine, our real self and with the creator who dwells within every atom of life. Becoming one within and without, with the creator within whom all things live and whose essence is all there is.

No spirit is able to manifest in the physical realm and experience life on earth except by their own volition. The force of life only flows onwards and no spirit is able to live in any dimension and in particular on the physical realm, in resistance to the life force, whatever that entity may think.

No living entity is 'made' to incarnate on the earth, in a state of punishment for some unknown misdemeanour in a past life, or is somehow 'not belonging' or 'didn't ask to be born'. Neither is it 'your' life. Life is all; it flows through you and you are life. You cannot own life, you can only live, because you are life and are inseparable from the life force, which is the creator.

The death process itself is in accordance with the natural flow of ever onward life energy. It is a natural shedding of 'skin' and a progression throughout many experiences of the force of life.

There is no cosmic judge or assessor of crimes. There is only perfect and absolute logic. The only law is that of cause and effect; that has, in human terms, taken on a moral aspect. Certain actions are what we term 'wrong', because they cause damage or an undesirable outcome to the perpetrator and generally to the recipient of these actions; the recipient being another human, an animal, the earth itself and so on. The moral aspect has developed naturally over time. There is no God showering down wrath from on high, in rage at the human species. The force of life is all and the laws of logic, cause and effect are complete. The process of humanity growing up, is a realisation and understanding the law of logic on every level. This is the active understanding that thoughts, emotions and finally actions have ongoing and corresponding results that are exact and unwavering. In simple terms, the result of what you have prepared to eat is made of the ingredients you have put into the recipe; it cannot create anything else. Humanity has a unique and surprising optimism, that we doggedly believe that different results can arrive despite, the ingredients in our recipes.

There is no 'Divine Retribution' meted out by a jealous God. Only the absolute law of cause and effect presides. This is one level of meaning concealed within the words 'an eye for an eye'; it does not mean if your eye is taken, go ahead and take out the eye of the guilty party. If that were the case then eventually the whole world would be blind.

It simply means that 'morality' is the pure and unwavering motion of cause and effect.

The answer is always the same, education; education in the laws of logic which propels the 'growing up' of humanity.

## The Question of Manifestation and Parallel Realities

To understand this we must go back to before the beginning; that darkness of the empty void, the silence of nothing. For nothing to 'be', it is at the same time 'existing' in its state of nothingness. The reality of nothing is an existence, and, therefore, is always in a state of dual realities. The realities of non existence, are so, because nothing exists. This is a simultaneous dual reality of non existence and existence.

From human perspective of creating and manifesting reality, the existence of the duality is easier to comprehend. The absence of something verifies the existence of it. The art is to combine with the existence rather than the absence. The dual reality of you, having the desired experience exists simply because it is wanted. The 'wanted' exists, because the 'having' already exists. It is a simple stepping from one experience into another. This is why experience, can change in an instant.

The Evolution of humanity is at one with the progress of science. The tentative steps into the understanding of the universe are only the beginning. The evolution of science will develop into the gathering of wisdom, not just in the physical world in which we live, but also way beyond, into the many dimensions of reality. The evolution of science is hand in hand with the 'growing up' of humanity; The journey of science is one of reaching out, way beyond the limits of physical knowledge into the causes of the infinite universe, that dwell in the infinity of logic itself and the absolute law of life.

# The Images of the Tarot cards

The origins of Tarot cards are arguable. The images and symbolism, however are clear, ancient and precise. They are part of the world's rich heritage of esoteric symbolism.

How do these images express the forces of creation and where are their places on the Tree of life?

Each Major Arcana card has long been associated with a Hebrew letter and a pathway on the Tree of Life. There are different opinions as to the correctness of which letter and path each card represents.

It is important that the age old symbolism of the elements has never been an ignorant misunderstanding of the physical world. This symbolism has always been the conveying of vast depths of wisdom and knowledge of the world in which we live and the formative dimensions of reality and of mankind's communion with his own spirit and every aspect of his being.

Fire is always the illustration of the Spirit; the one spirit of the creator and the divine spirit who dwells within every created essence. The spirit of life is referred to as light or fire, the Father or the bridegroom. This is the divine source of the human spirit.

Water is the symbol of the world of gestation, the universal soul; the mutable world of movement and sound reverberation. The water of life is the unconditional world of acceptance and complete love. This is also described as the divine Mother, the bride. The human soul is forever bound within this world and like water, every drop will one day be reabsorbed into the unity of the eternal divine ocean.

Air is the illustration of the communion of fire and water. It represents the son of the Father and Mother, the Spirit and the Soul. This is the region of communication, of formulation and intention. This is the region of thought. Air is described as the divine child, the son, perfect thought. Humanity is an expression of the son of the divine spirit and the sacred soul. The higher intellect of humanity is forever in harmony within this region of existence.

The son goes on to have children and is the creator of generations. As humanity develops consciousness, the lower mental body begins to form. It is the product of the higher intellect beginning to reach down into a differently vibrating reality. The thoughts become more selective and more specific and can also degenerate into doubt.

As the thoughts begin to become more manifest and close to our experience of physical reality, they begin to present as 'condensation'; a more fluid and mutable experience. These are expressed as emotions from a human perspective. These emotions may be lifted to commune with their counterpart in the higher regions of the soul or may sink lower into more densely felt negative realities.

Earth is the representation of the physical world. This is the symbolism of the daughter. Physical reality is created from a human point of view by the condensation of thoughts and emotions.

All of these regions exist in themselves and humanity flits with speed between these regions according to the direction of their thoughts and feelings. The higher worlds are connected to the lower realities and continually send their energy into them to, bringing with them the constant force of light, the essence of life and creation.

The lesser Arcana cards are more easily placed and understood.

Simply the 'aces' which represent the number one all belong to the first Sephira, Kether. The wands represent the Spirit and fire. The next, the cups represent water, the soul. The air, the product of the Spirit and the Soul, is symbolised by the swords. Finally, the Earth, the physical manifestation, is illustrated by the disks. Here we have four aces, depicting the number one that has four phases or dimensions of reality.

This is a clear way of understanding why it is said that there are four angelic beings surrounding the highest and most sublime region of Kether; the Hayot ha Kadosh. One with the head of a lion, the symbol of fire and the spirit, the next has the head of an eagle, the ancient symbol for water and the soul. The third has the head of a man, representing air; the realms of thought. The fourth has the head of a bull, symbolising the earth.

The two of the lesser Arcana again has four dimensions, fire, the wands, water, the cups, air, the swords and earth the disks; again representing the phases of existence gravitating toward physical manifestation. The two belongs in the second Sephira, Chokmah.

The original four divine beings in Kether pour forth their energy and bring about the next phase of consciousness. Therefore the original four plus four times the power of two, creates twelve. Here we see the twelve Mazaloth or phases of the zodiacal forces that will manifest physical reality.

The three, in its four aspects belongs to Sephira Binah.

The forces above combine adding their twelve powers to four times three, giving a total power of twenty four. This is the number of the twenty four elders, the Aralim, that dwell in Sephira Binah.

The four belongs in the fourth realm of

Chesed, in its four emanations. So the combined power of twenty four is added to the four fours, giving us the total of forty. This is number of the divine entities in Chesed, the Hachmalim.

The fives belong to Sephira Gevurah, once again in their four realities. The power of forty combines with five times four and gives us the number of Seraphim in Sephira Gevurah, sixty.

The six belongs to the centrifugal force of Sephira Tifaret. The four elemental realities again show us the phase of unfolding existence. The power of sixty combines with four times six and gives us a total of eighty four, this is number of the angelic hosts, the Malachim.

The seven resides in Sephira Netzach in it four elemental forms. The power of eighty-four combines to create, with four sevens, the number one hundred and twelve; the principalities, the elohim in Netzach.

The eight dwells in Sephira Hod in four states; the one hundred and twelve blend their power with four times eight and give us one hundred and forty four, the number of the Bnei Elohim, the blessed sons of God, in Hod.

The nine vibrates in Sephira Yesod in its four states of being. The one hundred and forty four powers add themselves to the four times nine and give us one hundred and eighty, the number of the Kerubim, the angels of Sephira Yesod that walk with humanity.

The ten dwells in the Earth, Sephira Malkuth, the Kingdom in its four realities. The one hundred and eighty powers combine with the four tens and create two hundred and twenty, the number of the Ishim, the glorified souls that tend the Earth.

The court cards also have their four states of being, of fire water air and earth. They are, in themselves an illustration of the phases of creation, the Kings being the Father, the Spirit and Fire; the Queens being the Soul and water. The Princes represent Air, the sword, the region of thought. The princesses illustrate the physical world, the disks and the Earth.

The King or Knight has four phases and is the King or Spirit of Fire, fire of fire and pure spirit. He is the King of wands. He is next illustrated as the King of Water, of cups, the Fire of Water or the Spirit of Water. He is the Spirit of the Soul's existence.

The next phase is the King of Air, the Spirit of Air, the Fire of Air. He is the Spirit of thought and symbolised as the King of swords.

The fourth phase the King of Earth, the Fire of Earth, the spirit of earth and of disks.

The Queens follow the progress of manifestation. The Queen of Wands is the Water of Fire, the Soul of the Spirit and of Fire. She is the Queen of Wands. Her next representation is the Water of Water, The Queen of Cups, pure

Soul. She continues her journey and becomes the Water of Air, the mother of the son, the Queen of Swords. She is the Soul of Air and of thought.

The fourth phase is the Queen of Disks of the Earth; she is the hidden Soul of the Earth. The water of the Earth.

The Prince has four stages of existence. The Air of Fire, the Prince or Knave of wands; he is the thought of fire itself. He is next shown as the Air of Water, the Prince of Cups. He is the thought of water and of the soul.

He then becomes his purest representation as the Prince of Swords, the Air of Air; pure thought.

Finally, he gravitates into the Air of Earth; the Prince of Disks. He has become the thought of the Earth.

The princess is the physical manifestation, the regions of that which we call 'reality'. Firstly she is shown as the Princess of Fire, of Wands, she is the Earth of Fire; the physical reality of the Spirit.

She is then depicted as the Princess of Cups, the Princess of Water; she is the earth of Water, the physical soul and water of the Earth itself.

Her next phase is the Princess of Swords, she is the Earth of Air .She has become the Earth of thought; thought in the physical realm.

Finally she is illustrated as the Princess of

Disks; she is the Earth of Earth; she is
the physical manifested universe.

The ancients used these elements to describe
the ever more compound and ever more
manifest progress of creation that led to
the material world in which we live.

These elements are phases of
creation and stages of reality.

All the Kings belong to the second Sephira,
Chockmah. This is region of God the Father.

The Queens all reside in Sephira Binah.
This is the Dark Face of contemplation
and receptivity, God the Mother.

The Princes or Knaves dwell in the centrifugal
force of Sephira Tifaret, the place of the
Christ and the Divine imagination.

The Princesses reside in Malkuth, the Kingdom.

Here we can see the image of a man, with hands
stretching up above his head. His head, his
thought in the centre of the Tree of Life and his
feet resting on the Earth. This is the symbol of
Christ, Crucified, on the great living Tree.

Living forces, that draw from the dimensions
of creation beyond them and commune
with their own unique Divine imagination
the Christ ignition, are the absolute logical
progression of the process of creation.

Humans often ask 'what is the meaning of life?'

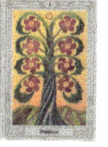

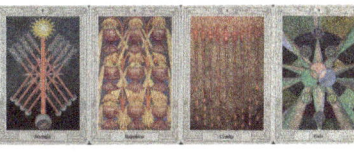
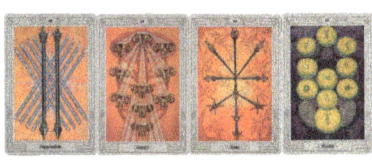

The meaning of life is creation. The meaning of creation is life.

# A Pause for Thought

It is important to understand that the symbolism and titles to explain the forces of creation are titles to vast tomes. The word Arch angel, or angel, for example, bare no relation to the illustrations of humanoid figures with wings with which we have become so familiar.

The term Arch Angel is in reality, a reference to what is an unimaginably powerful force of pure thought. The angels, or children of the archangel is a term that illustrates the condensation of the immense force of thought, that coagulates, through its own intense focus, into ever more manifest reality.

The symbolism of Kings, Queens Princes and Princess again is an simple illustration of vast forces of the creative process; the force of pure spirit, of the Universal Soul, of the forces of thought, produced by the Spirit and Soul in Harmony and the physical world that is the culmination of all these forces.

The pure force of what we describe as fire or light, by its velocity creates absolute focus, this in turn, propels a series of results, each state is the direct result of the precedent. The pinpoint or nucleus of light, created by the velocity of the spinning energy of fire, causes a reaction and resonance, that is described as the receptive Soul, illustrated as water. This is because water is receptive, responsive to emotion and retains memory. The combination of fire acting upon water, or the Spirit acting in harmony with its own integral result, the Soul, produces steam. This is a completely new entity, and it is this new result, that is described as 'thought' or the 'child' of the creator, or in Sephirotic terms the 'Archangel'. This is pure thought. Thought is a living being and the precursor of all levels of manifestation. All thoughts are living beings. As the thought becomes energised from the attention to which it is given, it begins to 'settle' in the same way as steam creates condensation. This may be described as 'emotion' and is illustrated as the 'children of the arch angel' or angelic forces. These descriptions have become ever more 'humanised' throughout the ages. The same series of phases apply to all creation and all manifestation.

# The Life of Number Forces

Number are living forces, made of
light and formulated by sound.

The unfolding steps of logic that create one force
after another are what we describe as numbers.
These are the poetic phases of numerical
birth, from which the vast matrix of energies
are formed. The forces which will later go on
to develop into our own physical universe.

The Eleventh Dimension

Let us revisit the instants of creation, the
Creator's voyage of discovery, that we may
conceive as the concept of numbers.

That moment of absolute arrival, of coming
into being, the Birth of God, caused by the
immeasurable momentum, whipping itself
into a vortex of energy, creates that poised
nucleus of apparent stability. The essence of the
moment of perfection, is the constant, perfect
and infinite instant of birth, of recognition,
of primal awareness. The recognition that
is illustrated by the sacred name Ehieh,
not yet "I am" but "I will be". This is all
that we understand as the number one.

The immense force of the creation of the
"lightening flash" shows us a "secondary"
force that is set forth on its explosive
journey, by all that is within the "one".

Because of this instant, a series of events are
instigated, by the force of energy formulated
by all that creates the number one. This force

causes the rippling effect of energy in circular waves eddying from its own essence to create the five self realisations, or dimensions, flowing from within itself; that are known as a Sephira.

This flowing of energy in itself is the number two.

Each and every time the principle of a nucleus is reached, it is not only the creation of a new Sephira, it is also an infinite number of "Tree of Life" formations set into process. So, within each Sephira, because of each point of creation, a never ending, eternal process of Tree of Life formation is realised.

The new discovery of direction develops the third experience or the number three. This moving away from the singular direction of the extension of the number one, that we call two.

This new discovery can continue onwards, but once realised has no other choice but discover a new self realisation. This is the return to the point of one by not repeating its journey, but by following the path of least resistance and returning directly to itself in the beginning moment of "one". This is the process of the number force that we call "four". The result of this movement, is the "five" the creation of flat surface. The building block of life; a space, ready to be ignited by the creative spirit. This reveals to itself the ignition of the spirit in to the empty space, the moment of "six". As we have seen these stages of self discovery continue their journey of perfect logic and create the first three dimensional formation; thus revealing the seven, the next instance of the ignition of the life force into matter. Thus revealing the three lines of formation, that create the four flat surfaces, creating seven possibilities. Later to be formulated as the seven visible light frequencies, the three primary colours and the four other colours, made up of the three original frequencies. Thus the principle of the four flat surfaces flows onward to create the eight, from its own essence of directional possibility. This is expressed by the figure eight that shows us the flowing of energies, of the that which is above is like unto that which below. This shows us the eternity and timelessness of existence. It shows us how we see small essences of what we see as time, is only a part of an endless ellipse. The whole journey of primal creation of the first solid is accomplished by nine stages. There are only nine numbers, nothing else exists other than nine numbers. Nine life frequencies and nine experiences of self realisation.

Thus the nine, however many times it is multiplied, it must always add to the number nine. The two sets of digits can only "borrow" from themselves in order to multiply.

$$1 \times 9 = 9$$

$$2 \times 9 = 18$$

$$3 \times 9 = 27$$

And so on. The counting process must begin again.

There we have the ten, which is made up of one set of nine and an empty space, the zero, ready to be ignited by the life force. This is the last Sephira, Malkuth, the physical world.

So, by watching the formation of each "number" force we can begin to feel the entire process of creation. Our own place, Malkuth, expresses itself, mathematically, as all that which is above, is like unto that which is below, in the phrase written on the Emerald Tablet of Hermes Trismegitus.

Following this process the next step of logic is to "ignite" the empty space by adding the number one into it. Adding the spirit into matter. This is the element of creation, or Divine imagination. The name of God Yad Hé Shin Vav Hé, or, in the western world, Jesus.

This Divine imagination, that which is the essence of the human state. All is thought, all is imagination, all is the exact image of the creator, the Divine imagination. The number eleven. This is predicted in the process of adding the one into the zero of ten.

Therefore, if that which is above is like unto that which is below, we can experiences the new process of counting, a repletion of events once more.

If we "add" the spirit into the zero, we

can express in this way , that the if the "one" that brings forth Sephira Kether contains all that will formulate in Malkuth, Sephira "ten" then 1=10. If we add the spirit "1" to the "10" we arrive with "11"

If we follow this process then "2" Chokmah =9, adding the "2" to the nine ="11"

Therefore "3" Binah ="8" and adding it, arrives at "11"

And so on through the Tree of Life, each Sephira having the possibility of "11", when we arrive at Sephiroth 5, Gevurah and 6 Tiphareth, a beautiful and elegant "DNA" shift occurs in the numbers , all doing an "about turn" as the numbers flow downwards and formulate the physical appears of matter.

The same elegance can be seen as it replicates in the counting together of the numbers in the pathways, revealing another poetic DNA shift as the secondary phases of static geometric energy formulates itself toward Malkuth.

Each number force is the creator of and the creation of a new dimension of experience.

Because each sephira adds up to 11 the counting process begins again indefinitely 1+1= 2 etc

So, each sephira automatically begins within itself its own infinite, holographic re creation of dimensions. As each nucleus re creates and self generates an infinite

Tree of Life matrices, the essence force and experience of becoming each Sephira deepens ever more profoundly and infinitely.

11 dimensions exist fundamentally each within itself an infinite creation of infinity mathematically.

Yad He Shin Vav He the ignition of the spirit into matter calls into being the process of infinite animated creation.

The K in Kabbalah is the 11$^{th}$ letter of both Hebrew and western alphabet and therefore reveals that Kabbalah with a K holds the keys of infinite dimensional creation.

Therefore

Each time a human thinks, they receive the living thought force, regurgitates it and compounds it in emotion and thus formulates it physically.

Each time a human adds their own life force to thought and sends it away to do its work, a new dimension of existence is created. Thus becoming the creator of realities and existences, i.e. dimensions.

The eleventh dimension of existence is the creator and the creation of the Divine imagination. The imagination which is the "christ" factor, God experiencing existence within the human state, within human evolution and within matter.

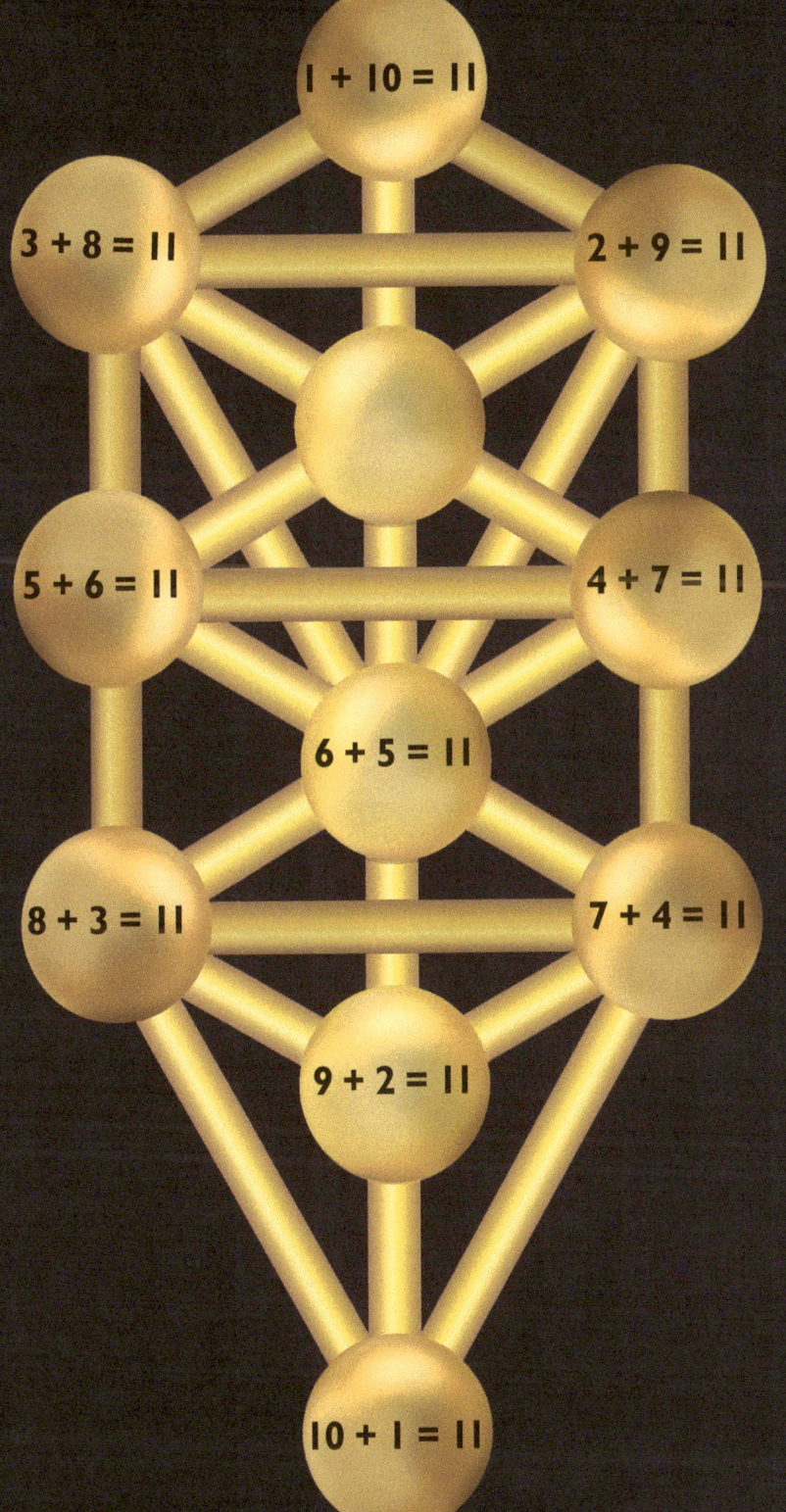

This is an astonishing moment of self discovery. This is the moment when humanity, the creators from perfect imagination and becoming the creators by perfect imagination come into their own potential. Each time a human thinks another dimension is born.

The expansion of the universe is so because of thought and human thought causes the momentum and the perception that time is speeding up from a human perspective.

This is the meaning of humanity being in the image of God.

The infinite and constant state of every aspect and phase of creation expresses that time does not exist, the past, present and future are simultaneous, it is not, what was, is and will be in a linear sense, but all at the same time, co-existing. To express it more simply, God and creation are all **now**.

The arrival at "one" is that exquisite moment of awareness; the first nucleus of perfect and focussed light, the moment of becoming and the Birth of God.

# The Eleventh Dimension

**The eleventh Sephira**

The possibility of infinity dwells within each Sephira, each nucleus of light is the catalyst of a journey of perpetual creation. Each Sephira contains the power within itself of all the numerical forces. Each Sephira equals the number eleven. This predicts the existence of an eleventh Sephira. This Sephira is the constant ignition of the spirit and the divine creative force of imagination. This Sephira is the source of all inspiration and the culmination of the 'Creator'. The 'adding' together of all that each Sephira contains is the addition of the Spirit within the Spirit, this causes a never- ending process of inspiration, imagination and because of this, creation of a never- ending discovery.

The epicentre of light that comes into being is described by the word YHSVH This is the sacred name of God. This is the addition of the letter Shin into the formation of reality, that has been formed by the word YHVH. This is known as the Holy Pentagramaton and has been handed down to us as the word Jesus.

This was not the name of a man, but is the sacred name of power, understood by Emanuel, the son of Miriam. This word is the secret name that unlocks he gateways to the creator within each human being. This is name of the divine imagination and the key to conscious manifestation.

Each letter forms the Holy Pentagram of the

initiate. The first line flowing from Chokmah to Binah, joining Wisdom and Understanding. The second line flows from Binah to Chesed, linking Understanding to Divine Love. The third line flows back to the summit of Kether, linking Chesed and Kether; joining together Love and Truth. The fourth line flows down from Kether to Gevurah, linking Truth and Power and the fifth line flows from Gevurah to Chesed, closing the pentagram between power and love. This is the human, perfected, at one with the Holy Star, the Magan David; that is expressed by the world of the Spirit, Aztiluth and the world of the Soul, Beryah.

Each sacred letter is a force that dwells within and is born from the Magan David.

The nucleus causes the motion of precession; the energy in a perpetual process of self-recognition. The Sephira Daath is created in a continual state of resonance. The word Daath can be understood as knowledge .This is knowledge of the power of the divine imagination within each human being.

The child of YHSVH and Daath, the name of God and the name of the Sephira, the Spirit and the Soul, the Father and Mother, is the Arch Angel of fire Lucifer, "the light of fire". The immense force of thought is the result of the union of the emissive and receptive states of being.

This is the Archangel that works incessantly with the divine imagination of humanity.

Expressing the laws of cause and effect, that cannot be manipulated or avoided. This angel has been seen as the harbinger of evil, the deliberate causer of all the ills of humanity. This is a childish perception. There is only the law of absolute cause and effect .The law of logic. The responsibility of each individual cannot be passed on to a fictitious entity that somehow 'made' a human do an act that will have ongoing and ill advised results; this the light of illumination and the fire of the spirit of creation. The human has the destiny of working with these forces, until they grow up into adulthood, realising their immense power, all propelled by the divine imagination within.

The children of the Arch Angel Lucifer are the entities that dwell alongside the lower thoughts and feelings of humanity. The disturbing and unwanted feelings that are a guide to the human; clearly marking the way by these unwanted thoughts and feelings. They say, 'this is not good, come this way', drawing them closer to their perfect and divine self, their 'real' self that dwells forever in Sephira Tipharet . The 'real' self can be awakened and felt by the communion with the sun's rays and breathing in the life force of the creator that is constantly pouring forth light and life into the physical world. These angelic hosts are called Oryot, "lights".

The physical force of the final wave of energy, that draws back and stabilises its force, creates the potential of the planet

Pluto; the most remote planet from Earth.

The pathways, letters and numbers

The potential of the stabilising phase of creation, caused by the dissolution and receding of energies back into their source, cause the secondary possibility of the formative process. The culmination of the numerical potential within each sphere of creation, adding to eleven, creates the existence of the eleventh Sephira.

This creates an infinite process of
Tree of Life formations; each born of
the nucleus from its own self.

Thus the progression of addition
begins its perpetual self creation.

The drawing back of energies, creates form and stability. The ten Sephirot are the primal and perfect resonations of the 'name' of G-d in an ever self-recognising voyage of discovery. The eleventh Sephira is the generation of infinite realities, that dwells within each nucleus of absolute light; the' name of God'.

The pathways affirm the matrix of creation, growing ever more dense, in energy, as they become nearer to the manifest world that we call reality.

The pathways are formed by sound, the result of light energy, the secondary wave or recognition of existence. The pathways reinforce the destiny of infinity. They begin their journey of counting with the number eleven, each digit adding up to next numerical possibility Eleven, therefore = 1+1=2, Twelve =1+2=3,

thirteen=1+3+4 and so on until they too reach the epicentre of Tifareth and do an beautiful DNA twist and become ever more dense as they formulate the illusion of material reality.

## A Brief Pause

The words Miriam and Joseph, are, in themselves, extremely important. Miriam is made up of the two Mem, the Soul, water in all dimensions of existence; the gestating womb. The two Mem, contain within, the immense wisdom of creation; bestowed through the hand of the Creator. They contain Air, the son, Divine thought. The Resh conveys the physical reality that will be born into the Earth.

The word Joseph, the Father of Emmanuel, is made up of the Yad, the hand of the Creator and the word Seph, "book" and "numeration". This implies one who has inherited, studied and understood the sacred ancient wisdom.

The bible tells us that "Jesus" or Emmanuel was born of three sets of fourteen generations of Initiates, all clearly named, who were descended directly from David the King.

# A Pause for Thought

The eleventh Sephira

It is when we see the Tree of Life in a three-dimensional structure, its perfection, dictated by the precise and poetic mathematical formulae, we can see the vital eleventh Sephira. The eleventh Sephira, the Christ factor, the Imagination of the Divine, is that which is the pivotal impetus of the entire matrix of energies; the energy of creation itself.

When we see this structure, before our eyes we can see thirty- three pathways. The thirty-three years of the life of the Christ, the thirty-three degrees of Freemasonry. Each pathway illustrated by a sacred letter, a number, a resonance. The twenty -two letters received into what has become the Hebrew Alef Bayt, the twelve additional finite letters and the unknown silent letter, that has been searched for and so long awaited, by generations of sages.

The Sephirotic three- dimensional Tree, shows us the vital importance of the three columns, which are born from the three forces that flow from the source of absolute light of the primal Birth of God. These flow onward and creating firstly, the principle of flat surface and then the first principle of solid and cohesive physicality. The Blessed Six, which contains within itself the keys of all creation, illustrates once more, the three pillars that descend from each corner. Three columns, that have been described for aeons by the sages and great masters.

Then we may see the eleventh Sephira, the moment of magic when zero, empty space, is ignited by the Divine Imagination and infinite creation begins its perpetual journey.

In three dimensions, the prism which is created in the centre of the Tree of Life structure, reveals the voyage of light, beyond our comprehension, that flows into the centre of the mathematical structure, that then graceful twists, and bestows its life force in ever condensing force, which creates the semblance of physical reality. This is the prism, which is contained, and lies in anticipation, within the Blessed Six, the primal solid and template for all creation.

The thirty-three pathways have evolved into physical reality, throughout three dimensions, to become tangible and all that we may experience in the physical world.

The simplicity and clarity within the Sephirotic Tree reveals the transformation of the Christ factor, the Divine Imagination, transforming into thought, then resonating with emotion and final condensing into physicality.

The eleventh Sephira describes the vital role of every human being, their vital journey of becoming conscious creators of universes.

# The Creation of Surface. God in three

This chapter expresses the simple phases of logic that create firstly flat surface and then the primal building blocks of all the possibilities that will later contribute to the apparent solid formation of the Universe.

How does our perception of physical reality form from the single point of absolute light and the quintessence of the Birth of the Creator?

An exercise

Take a blank piece of paper.

Rest a pen on its point anywhere of the page.

Spend some time 'being' this single point, this moment of 'I am'.

Become this moment suspended before time, become this eternal moment of awareness.

A moment will arise when you realise the potential of 'something' else. Of change from this point of 'I am'.

There is only one logical answer.
To move. To move forward.

Keeping your pen on the paper, move forward from the starting point.

This is the discovery of what will become 'future'. This potential is eternally within the starting point of 'I am' and is eternally 'I will be'.

The one has become two.

You have discovered direction.

This journey forward could go on endlessly, but logic dictates that nothing more can be discovered in an eternal journey forever forward. There is only one answer; to change direction.

Keeping your pen on the paper begin to change direction. It does not matter whether this is left or right, or even up and down. The process is exactly the same and will lead to the same discovery.

Continue forward.

Logic again would dictate that nothing new can be discovered by the journey in this direction.

You may continue a discovery of endless changes of direction, which would not add any new experience. Even 'circling' will not lead to anything new.

So logic again steps in and stops the journey, in order to discover another possibility.

There is only one answer, to accumulate your experience of the starting point and direction.

Change direction once more and head back to the starting point.

When your pen arrives at the original point, observe what you have discovered; flat surface.

Three directions of experience which have created a new concept.

The creator in three; the first
vital building block of life.

Within this triad or triangle, we see six directional lines of energy. Three nuclei created by four concepts; the beginning point, the first direction, the discovery of change of direction, the repetition of change of direction resulting in the return to the beginning.

The empty 'space' or flat surface
is the fifth discovery.

The starting point may be illustrated with the Holy letter Yad, the only Hebrew letter that exists, all other letters are an extension, a twisting a turning, a new discovery of the Yad on its journey. The spirit and the source of all.

The discovery of movement forward is illustrated by the Holy letter Hé. The creator of 'future'. The Mother, The Soul.

The change of direction is illustrated by the Vav, the symbol of which is the 'nail', the pivot point and is illustrated as an extension of its Father the Yad. The Vav, the son.

The final process the returning to source, is illustrated again by the Hé, the returning, the replica of the Mother, who creates future. The daughter creates the possibility of physical manifestation, by producing flat surface.

This is the entrance into the profound knowledge hidden within the letters Yad Hé Vav Hé, the

Holy Tetragrammaton. The sacred Name of God that gives birth to the third Sephira, Binah. The Holy name of God the Mother, the creator of physical reality. This name contains the entire process of creation and is God in three.

The 'space' or flat surface is a new reality; a new discovery, a new state of being of the creator. This is the fifth self realisation of the creator and is the primordial potential of physical life. The four sacred letters of the Tetragrammaton express the creation of 'space' and surface. The surface is ready to receive the ignition of light flowing from the source. Light allows the surface to be observed and recognised as a reality. This is expressed by the addition of the letter 'Shin' the Divine fire. The sacred name of God Yad Hé Shin Vav Hé, the Holy pentagrammton, expresses the illumination of being, the enlightenment of surface.

This is word that has transcended many generations and been handed down to the western world as 'Jesus'; this is the sacred name of the creator that was revealed to Emmanuel.

Every phase of this creative process is unplanned and arrived at by simple and absolute steps of logic. The momentum of movement that dwelled within Ayn Sof, continuing the journey of self discovery and recognition.

This primal journey is the principle of all that will become physical reality.

Each and every development is eternal and co exists. Each and every discovery and recognition is perpetual.

# Dimensions of Existence

Each phase is born from the source before it and it functions within its own unique quintessence.

Every nucleus of light, every vibration of sound and harmony, every matrix of energy every thought, emotion, every molecule, every atom of existence, all that is all, is the constant and perpetual self recognition of creator and the infinite Birth of God.

We have followed the process of the creation of surface, progression being a product of absolute and simple logic. The four stages reveal that in every aspect of the creative discovery, whether it be the universe or the realisation of our own thoughts, correspond to the same process of creating a dimension and then descending from that with a more and more condensed and reinforced version.

The first region of all creation is the impetus and ignition of the spirit. This caused waves of recognition and awareness, the second region of the receptive soul. Thought is released, the third dimension, known as the etheric regions, that have their own life and existence. The world of thought begins to descend as condensation, (or lower emotions), the astral dimensions. This world has the life force and power to accumulate and draw in energy in order to present the physical experience or 'reality'. These two dimensions are forever bound in magnetic response to one another.

The force and power harboured within the regions of thought and feeling together provide the elements with which the physical presentation is made. The most dense of all the dimensions of reality is the physical world in which we live.

# The Creation of the Physical Universe

Berashith

The discovery of flat surface, the process of the principle of surface is the first building block of physical reality. The whole journey can be seen in the life supporting chemical arrangements of $H_2O$ and $CO_2$.

The first triangle is made up of three power points at each corner creating six directional flows of energy. It has been formed by four stages of discovery. This tells us several simple things. The points and directions add to nine, the sum of the whole. The ten exists as the empty space created within the triangle. We can see also that the four stages of discovery have created three phases, the first surface, the triangle. This speaks of the three primary colours and the four secondary colours created by the communion of the original three. So we can see the principle of the visible light spectrum, within this initial state of discovery.

This journey of logic continues by connecting with itself in the least possible 'moves'. Following this voyage of discovery, the result is the first solid principle; that of the tetrahedron.

The tetrahedron is the embodiment of the triangle and all the discoveries it has accumulated. The original point (it does not matter which point to work from, as all is equal and the same) generates three directions of energy, resulting in twelve forces. These three nuclei create six lines of connecting energy. This is the Bera Sheta, Berashith, the Blessed Six.

Within this primal structure dwell
all the possibilities of life.

There are three nuclei

Six communing lines of energy

Twelve directional forces.

Four flat surfaces, illustrating that the
fourth dimensional world is 'visible' due
to the colour spectrum created by the
potential of the three and the four.

Within the Blessed Six many things can be seen.
The process of movement continues and by a
series of observing the 'turns' the tetrahedron
can make, we can see that a cross section reveals
two sets of eleven. It contains infinite creation
caused by imagination, by adding the one into
the empty space of ten. These cross sections are
perfect prisms, able to receive and emit light.

Within these turns we see the forces of polarity,
of magnetism and momentum. We see that
the tetrahedron contains within itself the Tree
of Life structure. It can also be observed that
the wisdom of that which is above is like that
which is below is hidden as two Tree of Life
structures in a state of perpetual suspension
and , at the same time, eternal movement.

The two elevens add to twenty two, describing
the twenty letters of creation, dwelling within the

Blessed Six. As the entire tetrahedron revolves the swirls of energy within it form the sound waves that accumulate as patterns or 'letters'.

By concentrating upon the tetrahedron and then looking once more at the Sephirotic Tree, we can now see that this is not a flat diagram, but is three dimensional. With this in mind it is clear that the top most supernal world is the tetrahedron. This shows us why the sages of old illustrated the diagram with three columns. There are three dimensional models which show four columns and the topmost region, resembling a pyramid. This is not the original template as it does not illustrate the journey of absolute light.

When we see the three dimensional tetrahedron as the supernal world, we see that it contains all the number process of creation, and all the potential of light becoming 'visible'; to see and be seen.

This then reveals that the centre of the Tree is also prism, where the light from the perfect moment of Ehieh flows down into the centrifugal Sephira of Tifaret and then completes the glorious DNA twist as it manifests as visible light, on its way to manifesting physically. The four Sephira that create the middle of the Tree of Life create the pattern of the pyramid, the pinnacle of Tifaret, the centrifugal point, which is the receptor of Divine light that transmits the creative force of light, which is life, into the regions beneath.

This then shows us that the lower worlds also create a tetrahedron, an exact image of all that is above.

When this process is perfected, it shows us that there are twelve Sephirot. The primordial ten; the eleven of divine imagination and infinite creation and the ultimate twelfth, created by the conscious joining of humanity to the creator; the voyage of becoming the image of the creator as a divine creator.

The Sephirotic Tree of Life is a matrix, created by infinite nuclei of focussed light. This is a holographic matrix of infinite prisms; receiving and emitting light that becomes ever more focussed and ever more manifest. The manifestation light appears to be physical and stable because of the continual, self generation of momentum and the elegant, perfect turn and about turn of the infinite vibrations of creation.

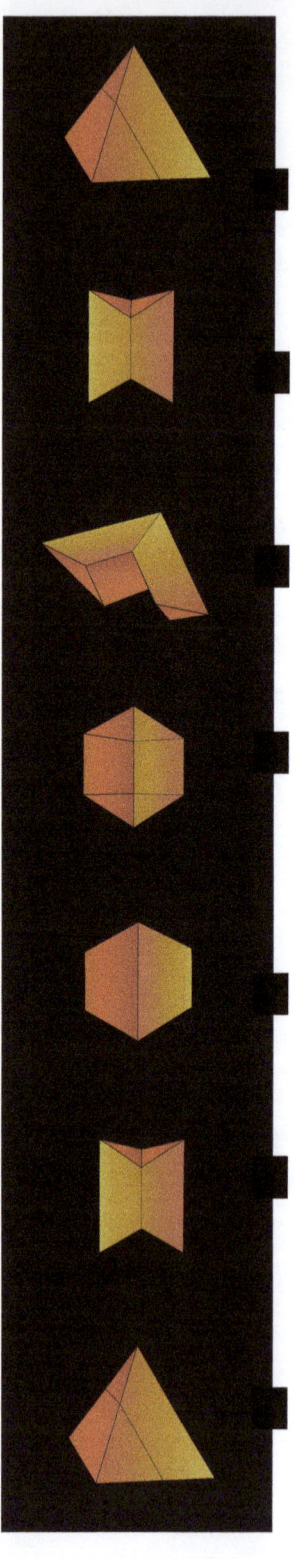

The topmost triad, the template of all that unfolds within the Tree of Life, is contained within the first tetrahedron. In three dimensions the top of the Tree of Life is a tetrahedron, a three-sided pyramid; from this tetrahedron flows the three pillars of creation.

By turning the two equal parts of the tetrahedron, we observe polarity

We observe the magnetism of the two sides being fused together

Here as the tetrahedron folds back, the first Tree of Life pattern may be observed within

The next turn of the two equal parts reveals again the Tree of Life pattern, expressing the for the first time the principle of "That which is above, is like unto that which is below"

The final movement expresses the sum of all the possibilities of the tetrahedron are equal to the whole and are contained within it.

We see a cross section, the unfolding of all that the tetrahedron contains.

# A Pause for Thought

The primal solid, the tetrahedron, created
by perfect light, contains perpetual
movement, never ending music and
the eternal word of creation.

Within it we can see six movements. The first,
showing the principle of polarity. The second,
magnetism and the law of attraction. The
third, the unfolding of the Tree of Life matrix.
The fourth replicates the matrix, revealing
that which is above is like unto that which
is below. Like unto, but a mirror image.

The fifth repeats the principles of polarity,
contained within all living things .The
sixth movement brings the solid back
to its original form once again.

The movement that is eternally active within
the tetrahedron is created by the energies
splitting into a perfect cross section. Thus,
creating the possibility for the Divine and
the Physical worlds to live in harmony.

The cross section within in the Blessed Six are
prisms, Both made up of six power points and
eleven lines of energy flowing from them.

This reveals the numerical pattern of physical
reality, that flows from this primal source.

# The Three Key Numerical Forces

The three, the six and the nine
are the keys to creation.

The first precession, the circular waves of sound energy, the effect of each nucleus of light, are the first expressions of this. A circle has three hundred and sixty degrees. The three and the six equal nine. However many times the circle is cut into a cross section, the degrees will always add up to nine; the sum of the total is always equal to the whole. The nine, however many times it is multiplied will always consist of numbers adding to nine.

This pattern continues in the infinite geometrical patterns of creation.

The three is the first discovery of surface. Each corner of the first flat surface, the triangle, expresses six directions. This describes the next phase of self discovery, the forming of the first solid, the tetrahedron. This first solid contains all formulated sound vibrations, created by movement. The nine is the ultimate destiny of number, the sum of the total, always being equal to the whole. Three forces of geometry harnessing the light and sound energy and formulate the physical appearance of the universe. The first energy is a dynamic mutable, swirling force that may be described as dynamic geometry; this is the untamed force of the spirit of life and creation. The second force is the harnessing of energy and the stabilising of the creative forces; this may be given the title of static geometry. This is the drawing in of energy, the patterns formed as 'letters' or language. This creates the framework or geometrical patterns that are observed everywhere in the physical world. The third geometrical experience is the infinite repletion of these forces, and is described as fractal. This is the holographic repetition of patterns that may be seen throughout our world of nature. These are the result of the self generating formulations of the Tree of Life matrix, perpetually born, as each new nucleus of absolute light is incessantly formed. This is a continual self creation; a holographic, infinite experience of self discovery.

## Golden Ratio

The golden ration is caused by the immense energy of the first vortex of light that brings into being the absolute pin point or nucleus of light. This is a process which constantly self replicates within all the aspects of the Sephirotic Tree. It is within the precession of the sound waves of the formation of each Sephirot. The Golden Ratio resides within the first tetrahedron as the energies within swirl and begin to form the first letter formations that reverberate with precise sounds. The process of creation of the first surface and then the first solid, the letters Yad He Vav He, the sacred name of God called the tetragrammaton quite literally, 'calls' creation into being. When the human voice replicates this and sounds this word, the nature of reality can change.

The Golden Ratio continues its journey of creation and can be seen within the geometry of sea shells, plants, mountains and every aspect of the cosmos.

# Atoms and Physical Existence

With all that has been described in mind, the question that naturally occurs is how does our personal existence manifest? How does it appear to hold together?

This process of the constant and perpetual Birth of God; how does this relate to our own reality?

The force which allows atoms to commune and become an individual being, of any kind, is movement. Movement begins its journey because of the existence of nothing, nothing that can only be recognised because of the existence of its polar opposite, 'something' or 'everything'. These are the two coexisting polarities that will go on to unfold and develop, into many ever more manifest presentations.

Each moment of arrival, or coming into being or experience is observed; recognised. There are two aspects that co exist; movement and observation. Every atom behaves differently when it is observed. It recognises its own existence by observation. All that makes up the atom, dances gracefully around each other. Movement harnesses them together, in the illusion of physical 'surface'. The force of light is the observer, the light that has been given the name the spirit; the source of light itself, the creator. Each atom of our personal existence is part of this perpetual 'dance' of the universe and part of the eternal recognition and is the one observer and is the observed. Light enables us to see and to be seen.

On every level and dimension of existence each individual is in constant communion with seeing and being seen.

Whatever world we commune with at any given moment, we are at the same time experiencing it and being experienced. Our level of consciousness and the vibration of our individual field of energy attracts 'magnetically' our experience, our attention to this experience reveals it to us and makes us both the seer and the seen.

Each tiny individual existence, whether it be an atom expressing the illusion of a grain of sand, a blade of grass or a minute insect is alive; alive because it is seen. Everything that we see, the grandiose and the minute is alive, made up of oscillating atoms. Life, which is light, is the unfolding of the creator; experiencing, observing and recognising. 'Seeing and seen'.

# The Qliphot and Dark Forces

All evil is born of doubt

According to the Bahir

Each Sephira is said to have its opposite, the shadow cast by the Tree of Light

A shadow can only exist in light

Humanity is born with a lower nature; these are the bodies that carry us through life. It is the purpose of humanity to learn how to tame these wild animals and to teach them to the will of our higher bodies; the real and perfect version of ourselves. This is the journey of evolution, the journey of becoming an adept creator, through the communion with our own "perfect version" of ourselves. This perfect version communes ever deeper within the human consciousness and at the same time is forever expanding in the many dimensions of existence beyond the physical universe.

As we learn and accept the responsibility of our own power, the limitless power of creation on all levels, we begin to create less chaos in the physical world.

Since the dawn of time humans have believed there to be evil entities, hiding in the darkness, waiting to pounce. These ideas were based upon very real fears, in the primeval world. As time passed, these fears, once associated with real threats, took on a more and more sophisticated form. But as thought and emotion create our reality, so our thoughts began to create egregors and thought forms and astral beings of malevolence. These demons exist only in the dimensions of fear, and are fuelled and given life by humanity. A shadow does not exist in the darkness. The darkness is not evil.

Animals who also have emotion also add to this dimension of fear. This follows, that when humanity evolves beyond eating or harming animals these dimensions lose their fuel significantly. In other words, stop the perpetuation of fear.

It is a normal and natural part of evolution to progress and work with thought and emotion and to arrive at a level of creating only in the higher dimensions and not creating fear and all the myriad of undesirable thoughts and emotions.

Within fear lives a multitude of entities.

The entire concept of evil and evil entities exists due to the thoughts and emotions of humanity, first at a primeval level and lastly at a sophisticated and intricate level.

Thoughts and feelings are living entities, and are created and fuelled by humanity. A thought or feeling, once emitted from the source, is drawn to and draws to itself its magnetic counterpart. These frequencies accumulate with astonishing speed and gather together within the corresponding dimension of existence, growing and gathering in force, taking on an existence that becomes more and more dense and more and more "real". Its only reality is the reality of its own make up and all corresponding frequencies of thought or emotion. It becomes the perpetrator and absorber of all thoughts and emotions that commune with the same frequency; feeding on and energising itself with the energy and life force of these corresponding thoughts and emotions.

This is true on all levels, both highly connected to the spiritual dimensions of purity and vibrant life and throughout the lower dimensions of destructive thought and emotion.

It is the purpose of humanity to learn the power of their thoughts and emotions and to learn to think and feel responsibly. This is the ultimate goal of every human being. There is no battle between the forces of good and evil. The life force within all things on every conceivable level is the one force, the one energy of the creator and of creation. Humanity and all living entities are both the creation and creators. Humanity has arrived at a remarkable summit of evolution and is rapidly casting off old ideas of reacting only to circumstance. Every moment of every day the human species is moving steadily and inevitably into adulthood, accepting their responsibility and realising the immense power of their thoughts and emotions.

The only demons to be vanquished are the entities that will ultimately be starved out of existence, by depriving them of their food source. The more we begin to devote our attention to the creation of all the goals and dreams of a united and elevated world, the weaker and more impotent our own demons and the collective demons of humanity become.

Evil exists only in the limited dimension of the lower human consciousness, the state of war and conflict is a reflection of the immaturity of the human species. Humanity is not so much "waking up" as "growing up". The transformation of the world in which we live, is the evolution of the species, the transition into responsibility and adulthood.

The Leo/Aquarius axis is the age we have recently entered. Predominated by the heat of the spirit (Leo) and the cold of the intellect (Aquarius). This age has yet to reach equilibrium and is predominated by the wild pendulum swing of these forces. Many are motivated by the heat of the spirit, resulting in unwise acts of the spiritual zealot; daily life is subjected and controlled by the etheric planes, of the Aquarian influence. Thus the world is dominated by "air borne" traffic, air flight, the internet, the media. Gradually, over time, a natural balance will be reached. The growing up of humanity will prevail. The evolution of collective and peaceful behaviour will become the norm. All the stark representations of selfish immaturity, in our personal lives, our governments, our media, our selfishness to the planet and to the universe in which we live, will, without doubt, transform. Humanity will look back at the planet's history as we now look back in wonder at the voracious dinosaur.

How can each individual contribute to this? The answer is simple and practical; take responsibility. Make responsibility your priority. Take responsibility for your emotions and your thoughts will swiftly follow the direction that you give them. Learn to be selective. Choose to accept only things that elevate your feelings into a better place. This does not mean ignore the things that need to be changed in our lives and in the world. Do not give your attention to the problem, only to the solution. Where there is war, then give your attention to peace. Give peace as much attention individually in your thoughts and collectively in your actions as possible. Where there is greed, give generosity your attention. Give generosity as much attention as possible, individually in your thoughts and collectively in your actions. Follow this formula in every aspect of life and you will be part of the changing world and an essential part of the evolution of your planet and of the universe. Think how quickly this transformation can happen, if every person decided to take responsibility.

# Death

The force of life is a constant momentum, this includes the death process. The death process is a natural shedding of all that has become stagnated in matter. This is sometimes difficult for the human psyche to reconcile, especially when the person who has died is 'young' or in our own perception 'taken' too soon. This is never the case. Each individual has their own momentum and their own journey of life. Life and death are constant, eternal and part of the same force. Each and every atom is eternal and has an infinite journey.

To be born physically, a spirit must pass into the most manifest regions of existence; the spirit 'dies' on the higher planes and steps into life in the physical world. When the spirit dies in the physical realm, it is born in the higher regions of life and becomes more intensively alive. The spirit continues its cycle of life, death and rebirth throughout many incarnations, gradually becoming more and more adept in its humanity and more adept as a conscious creator. The spirit celebrates its individuality and also its place as part of the collective; its unity with the source of light frequency, the Creator, and with the Soul, (which is recognition and the source of harmony), is eternal. Their quintessence, their 'true' self, dwells forever in the highest regions of Tifaret. Only a fragment of this infinite true self descends into life on the physical realm, the rest is constantly in union with their divine existence.

This 'true' self welcomes back its energy

when it is born again in the higher vibration of the Sephirotic Tree, after death.

The experiences of the lower emotional and lower mental worlds, throughout physical life are sometimes difficult for the personality to process. The lower emotional or astral worlds in the more dense regions of Sephira Yesod are inhabited by many entities, bound up with unfortunate feelings and destructive thoughts. For these personalities, time, space and concept of awareness other than the pain and confusion that they have created, does not exist. They are completely immersed within these emotions. This is their entire reality. There is a continual opportunity for these entities to escape this experience; there is a constant ebb and flow of the life force pulsating and generating momentum, which will enable the personality to evolve onwards and rejoin their own individual 'real' self, who dwells in the highest spheres. Eventually the emotion and lower thought will become worn out, by the constant replaying, which frees the entity to flow onwards within the life force.

This is an illustration of why suicide is never the best solution to a problem. Whilst the person is still in the physical body, they are at least, in some way, protected from the raw and engulfing emotions of the astral world. Once they are released from the physical body, they are totally sucked into the very emotions that they had wished to escape. It is very seldom that a person who has chosen this route can avoid this problem. The solution to this is education. Humans need to be better educated in the reality of death and the progression of life beyond. By learning how to manage and decide upon our emotions and lower thoughts; by deciding to take responsibility and to live a life of decision, instead of a reactive existence, these unfortunate actions and even more undesirable repercussions may be avoided. The good news is that life itself takes over and is unavoidable. The death and birth process is one of constant pioneering and evolution. There is no hell or purgatory or punishment, other than our own discovery of the laws of cause and effect. Humanity is always a participant and always an integral part of the whole. We do not have to desperately look for eternal life; we already are part of eternity and forever part of life.

Death on the physical plane is the natural process that takes place eternally and is a constant echo of initial the shattering of the vessels; the process of the primal Tree of Life becoming able to be suspended within a constant state of receiving and giving out of light and sound vibrations. The shattering of the vessels is the key to life on the physical plane. Death is a shattering of the vessel, the container, the body. This occurs when the forces of spirit, and the soul become too great to be contained within the body. The life of the spirit and the natural voyage of the soul are in a constant ebb and flow; in accordance to all the laws of logic within the Tree of Life. The infinite force of the spirit can only be contained within the body for a period of time, when the force becomes over full, the container must shatter, give in to physical death, so that the spirit may fuse once more with its immense essence high within the centrifugal Sephira of Tifaret, the source from whence of physical light and life cascade incessantly into the physical world. The soul, like water, is bound within a cycle of absorbing, it is immersed once more, within the universal soul and world of divine reverberating harmony.

This raises the question 'do we have the right to take away a life?' There are several things to consider. Firstly and most importantly, life continues eternally, but our personal cycles of the most manifest experience of life in the physical world need to reach their conclusion and full experience. By ending a life prematurely, for instance through euthanasia, it may be kinder from a human, short term perspective. However it must be seen from a far greater point of view, the person may have been released from suffering, but there may still be a short period belonging to the life cycle still to complete. This can lead to the spirit and soul of this individual incarnating soon after the event and living only for a very short period of time; causing great distress and suffering to the parents who have lost this spirit in the form of their child. It may be that with this knowledge, humans will begin to make different choices and assert their free will with clarity of the long term and ongoing effects of these decisions.

This also raises the question of 'should we keep life going artificially?' When we begin to understand that this one physical life is not the be all and end all and that it is a living eternal spirit that is being imprisoned in a body that would have surrendered to a natural death, our perception would be different. Many would not condemn a person to an indefinite suspension between the earthly and astral regions.

Only by understanding the whole cycle of events will we be able to make truly informed choices over life and death.

How may we commune with loved ones who have died? The vital thing to grasp is that our loved one, the 'real' self, the best version of the individual dwells always in the higher realms. This integral person cannot be found in sadness and grief. These things belong to us, whilst we are connected to the lower world of emotion and lower thoughts. We need to feel our loss in the physical world, to mourn. When the first shock waves and grief have abated a little, we can certainly begin to make our way toward the loved one, who is not lost and is easily rediscovered. This person cannot be found in unhappiness or anything connected to the lower experiences of life, as they are no longer there. By beginning to tend to our own feelings and beginning to find anything that raises our own emotions to a higher level, we may begin to commune with the best and real version of the person we wish to find. By imagining the very best version of ourselves, which is only a tiny fragment of the 'real' us, we are able to then imagine the best version of our loved one. This then brings the two spirits into communion with one another. In this way a closer and unbreakable bond may be forged.

# Reincarnation

Every human begins their voyage of physical experience by incarnating on the earth as one single celled amoeba of life. The instant the will of the human in the higher dimensions of existence expresses its destiny of completing the physical journey, this primitive aspect of life begins this long voyage of discovery. The intense, vibrating being that dwells in Sephira Tifaret and absorbs the euphoria within the immensity of the infinite dimensions of light, divides and shares a minute part of its essence. This fraction of its spirit descends downward throughout the regions of the Sephirotic Tree, finally making the journey through the more dense physical regions, passing through the pathway of forces of Scorpio. This is the 'fall' of man, who must encounter the physical forces of nature in order to incarnate. The fragment of light eventually arrives on the physical plane and begins its first experience of a single cell, a tiny pulsating being of physical life.

The tiny primal being goes through many incarnations and discovers many differing aspects of life in the gradually evolving animal kingdom. Each incarnation is a logical continuation of the previous life and experiences. At last the being will arrive at a human incarnation and begin its forming of human experience. The evolution of the human species is en mass a clear reflection of this process. Evolution of any species is exact and a result of cause and effect; the law of logic. There is nothing missing from the human story; there is no 'missing link' to be explained by a mysterious visit from an alien world. This step can be equated to a subtle genetic 'mutation', its origins barely traceable to the first individual to display this 'mutation' or evolutionary necessity to adapt and change. This change or evolution is propelled by the movement or journey of discovery of the pioneering spirit, that dwelled in the higher regions , expressing this movement by the physical genetic 'mutation' or development of a new direction of evolution. The mutation itself that may be seen in every species is a reaching forward, a branching out in a genetic sense. The Father and Mother stems, produce a third shoot, creation again replicating the creator in three. The third shoot is new, beginning a new direction of discovery and evolution.

The human begins to evolve from a basic and primitive mind into a gradually more and more evolved and intellectual being. This is reflected in the behaviour and values of each individual, as they learn the laws of cause and effect. Even the food they choose to eat is a reflection of this evolutionary progress. A human essence does not go 'backward' in incarnation into the animal world, but may sometimes become 'stuck' in the astral, lower emotional and lower mental regions in between incarnations. Their resistance to the life force and its progress is slowed down by immersing themselves in destructive feelings and negative thoughts that prevent their health and vibrancy from developing.

Eventually the human begins to accept their

immense power and realises that they alone create their destiny and that this is created by their own fabulous and unstoppable divine imagination. This is the moment of 'growing up' and stepping into their own aspect of God and their own Divine Power. At this extraordinary moment, the human begins to embrace once more their own magnificent and infinite 'real' self that is now on a voyage of conscious creation.

# Birth Reincarnation and Karma

The essence of the Creator is one of constant and perpetual division from an infinite source. Each individual life is made up from this eternal division. Each human entity has its source within each dimension of existence. Each human entity has its own eternal source and carries out its own infinite division.

As an entity begins its descent through the dimensions of life, it divides a small part of its being, which then begins its voyage throughout the dimension until it reaches the most dense and concentrated awareness of the physical world.

The greatest part of the vast and ever-expanding spirit of the individual remains within the world of light, of the spirit of the creator. Only a fragment of its essence separates and begins its journey into the physical realm.

The soul responds, resonates and recognises the fragment of life that has begun its descent. The immense and infinite soul, which is a perpetual state of constant multiplication, drawing its' essence from the infinite source of life, the eternal spirit, joins this descent. A fragment also leaves its eternal source and fulfils its process of "feeling" the experience.

The process of physical incarnation is then further verified by the Higher Intellect. The dimension of the eternal divine imagination, the essence of all human consciousness. The divine fragment, the Christ factor, joins the process of life.

The source of all three fragments remains in a perpetual communion within the dimensions of existence from whence it came. In actual fact, the division itself is an illusion and all reality is indivisible form its source.

The voyage continues through the lower etheric, mental planes of thought and then into the astral world of emotion. Throughout this process the entity gathers around it ever more dense vibrations of energy until it is finally resonating at a frequency that is a magnetic match to the physical realm.

When a child is born, it brings with all the experiences of its eternity. Much is said about the Karma of an individual and also of past life memories. Karma is simply the law of cause and effect. It has no relation to punishments or even paying a debt of some kind. The memories of the past are stored in the dimension of both Higher and Lower thought. As the entity reaches the denser energies of the Lower Etheric planes and the even more condensed regions of the Astral world of lower emotion, the memories and feeling become stronger and less objective. Sometimes a child is able to recall a past life with clarity for several years of their life, as, in some aspects, they are closer to these memories than to the present.

These memories in no way are able to damage the Spirit, Soul or Higher Intellect of an individual, it is only in the lower bodies that the person can be distressed. No human can incarnate against their will, as it is the will, the impetus of each spirit to create life continually. Sometimes an individual can become so immersed in their lower thoughts and emotions that this is hard to accept.

Through a process of incarnation and experience, the individual evolves to a conscious and glorious understanding that they have the ability to choose; to make conscious decisions and govern the laws of cause and effect. This is their "growing up"; their stepping into their true and divine purpose as creators, as one and in harmony with the source of all creation, that dwells within.

At this moment, a human begins to walk upright on the Earth.

# Revisiting the Human who Dwells within the Tree of Life

There are many ways to explain the make up of the human being. This one of the most clear approaches.

The human has a higher and a lower nature. It is easiest to split this up into six different functions. The term lower nature does not mean 'bad'; it is used to explain the way in which it functions at a more basic level of existence.

Each body reacts in a different mathematical way.

The lowest body, the physical learns to add up. In other words, it adds food, air, light and so on, in order to stay alive in the physical world. It says 'I want' or adds up.

The next body is the lower emotional body which also 'wants' or adds. It says I want love, respect, company, joy etc.

When either of these bodies are unable to 'add up' or get what they want, it is a very uncomfortable feeling. The human will 'jump' quickly into the next body; the partner in crime, if you like, of the astral body. The lower etheric or lower mental body then reacts by subtracting. It says 'that's no good', this is terrible' and when it gets really carried away it says something along the lines of 'there is no God!' 'God is a baddy and shouldn't let this happen' and so on.

When we try a little harder to overcome a situation or find a solution we cross the border line into the higher nature. The first body to take up the message is the Higher Intellect.

This body multiplies. It takes an idea or a thought and reaches outward, looking for a solution. It might even say 'this is not God's fault, it is humanity or even mine. Let me see what steps I can take to find a better solution'.

The next body is the Soul or the Higher Emotional body. This body is only able to multiply, to give out. This is the pouring out of unconditional love; in fact, true love is only unconditional. True love never says 'I want' it can only give.

If a person says 'I love that man or woman. I want them because I love them' they are not loving. They are only saying 'I want' and this is the astral body making demands, it is not the Soul. The Soul has no needs, it only gives out abundantly. It is not true that a soul can be damaged, lost or sold or in any way destroyed. The lower bodies may feel that they have been treated badly, but the soul is eternal and invincible.

The highest body is the Spirit, this is only able to divide, it divides its energy constantly and incessantly amongst the other bodies of the human. The source of the spirit is the source of life, divine light and part of the entirety of creation, at one with the Creator. A spirit can never be damaged, crushed or in any way spoiled, it too is invincible and eternal.

By simply imagining the very best version of ourselves that we can, we immediately begin to feel our way back to this Higher Nature, or 'real' you. The lower bodies learn, in time and discipline, to do their job and cease to dictate the life and experiences of the individual. By following the laws of cause and effect, we begin to take a proactive and decisive stance and learn the power of our thoughts and emotions. We learn to commune with our Higher Self, the 'Real you' and become less reactive beings and more and more focussed creators.

The lower bodies of men and women all carry out the same mathematical functions of adding and subtracting, but behave differently.

The physical body of a man emits and gives out and also adds up. The physical body of a woman is receptive and adds up.

The astral, lower emotional body of a man is receptive and adds up. That of a woman adds up and emits.

The mental body of a man subtracts and emits. That of a woman subtracts and is receptive.

Here we can see the age old problem between couples when they are determined to dwell in the lower nature. The woman often gives out huge amounts of emotion, wanting the man to reciprocate .The man cannot give out in this way, and is forced to 'swallow' all the tides of emotion, as he cannot help but 'add up'. He will soon feel that he is drowning. To escape this fate, he will jump into the lower mental body and immediately begin to subtract; he will emit negative mental statements, energies and thoughts, that the woman will have no choice but to receive and will begin to subtract internally, in thought.

In couples of the same sex, it is easy to see how the function of the lower bodies can carry out an equally unsatisfactory role. Only by caring about our feelings and cleaning up how we feel can we, through happier emotions and thoughts can we find our way back to a communion with our own 'real' self and harmony will once more be restored.

The human propensity to use various drugs and alcohol in order to change their state of mind, in itself is linked to the deeply rooted connection to wishing to commune with other regions of existence and their own integral highest aspect of being. In many instances it has become denigrated into avoiding reality or into a dumbing down the senses. No matter what substance is involved, it cannot, because it is physically sourced, connect or open up higher dimensions of reality in anything other than a momentary illusion or unsustainable way.

Each substance has a connection to a different dimension of the lower nature, according to its make-up and manner of consummation. A brief example is alcohol, which is fluid. The nature of alcohol, being liquid, affects the astral, lower emotional or fluid based body. Alcohol opens up and activates the lower emotional astral body, which very often begins to add up incessantly;

demanding more and more. The emotional body becomes more and more uncontrolled and demanding in response. This, in turn, attracts the energies within the emotional lower regions, gathering together, in a constant union that creates an emotional all devouring swamp. Cannabis, for instance, when smoked, activates the lower mental body and may, therefore create immobility, as this body subtracts and diminishes energy. Smoke is etheric and communes with the lower etheric regions and the lower mental body. Because of this, it is likely to cause paranoia, or doubt, the product of the dwelling in the lower etheric regions.

Each drug has its own individual connection with the human bodies and with the different regions of existence. This is not a matter of morals. It is an aspect of growing up, taking responsibility for the exact result of our actions. It is not sensible or intelligent to expect a different outcome from any substance other than that from which it is made. It is not a matter of a childish assertion of the right of personal choice or freedom; it is a simple understanding of the exact consequences connected to each substance.

The process of incarnation and evolution has brought us all to where we now are in our lives. This is true of our bodies and even the features on our faces. Never at any time has 'God made a mistake'; we are a direct result of our own experiences. It may be that some are deeply distressed and uncomfortable in their own skins and it is entirely that person's business as to what they decide to do to rectify that. These can only be partial measures, however, if the solution is only physical. The only path toward true happiness is the meeting and communing with the 'real' most perfect and fabulous version of the 'self' that can possibly be imagined.

This does not mean that someone who has disabilities or disfigurements have done something 'bad' in a past life. Very often these people are individuals of immense rarity and strength who have reincarnated in situations of great difficulty. They have a role to teach humanity and have the courage, joy and vibrancy of spirit to have taken on that life.

The situation of another has absolutely nothing to do with anyone else. Neither has someone else's opinion, thoughts, words or deeds, anything at all to do with us. The most useful technique is to 'mind your own business'. Each and every time we feel that we are straying into someone else's opinion of us, for instance, simply say 'mind your own business'. This not only tells us to stop involving ourselves in what doesn't belong to us, but also reminds us that something is 'our' business.

Our business is to care about how we feel. To love, care and tend for our own feelings and thoughts. Our business is to get as close as we can to that fabulous 'real' version of ourselves as we can. In this way we learn to care about what we feel and what we think. In this way we begin to understand the laws of cause and effect. In this way we learn the art of creation.

The most effective way to commune with the higher nature or 'real you' is , the minute you begin to feel in any way disturbed or unhappy, to find five things to help someone else feel better. Find five different things for five different people; think about this and carry it out. These five thoughts, feelings and actions will instantly lift you away from the lower regions in which you have been dwelling and will instantly connect you to the bodies that multiply and divide.

# The Future

Humanity has a unique and extraordinary purpose. Each and every one of us has a destiny, a destiny of our unique, individual creation. The purpose of humanity is to become "the image" of God; to become creators of our own Universe. Our creation is limitless; infinite.

By accomplishing our evolution as creators, with our own unique and Divine imagination, the Christ factor, the God, which is within us and is the life force itself, we accomplish the purpose of the Creator.

The logical and infinite progression of the Birth of God.

# The Creation of the Twelfth Sephira

As every individual accepts their own responsibility and their own power, they add to the formulation of the ultimate Sephirotic structure. The creation of the twelfth Sephira. This is the creation of and the result of the Christ factor in each human being. The twelfth Sephira transforms the Tree into a perfect symmetrical structure. A new Jerusalem, the twelve gates of light that also resonate the perfect musical scale. The new Jerusalem, that can also be observed in the human body.

It is humanity that calls into being a new nucleus of perfect light, a new aspect of the Spirit of God, the new "Name "of God. The ultimate possibility of perfect mathematical creation. I am Aleph and Tav, all is "nailed" to the cross, the Vav. I am all that is, was and will be, all at the same moment, constant and infinite.

Aleph, Tav, Vav. The hidden knowledge of the **ATU**. The twelfth Sephira, the perfect crystalline formation, that is created by light and transmits light to constantly create.

The meeting of the visible light spectrum, the fusion that manifests as Magenta. A unique frequency, where ultra violet and infra red become absorbed into each other.

The name of the Sephira, the soul, the resonance of sound, **Jerusalem**.

The name of the Arch Angel, the living spirit **Melchizedek**.

The name of the angelic hosts **Bnei Ishim**. The physical aspect **le Olahm**.

Each infinitely minute aspect of creation, within each atom of existence in the unfathomable dimensions of creation is absolutely unique and vital. On its own extraordinary journey of creation. All is part of the creator, the thinker, and all is the thought and the creator by thought. To have evolved to a human existence is a momentous achievement. These are only the first tentative steps toward becoming the image of the creator within each minutiae of existence.

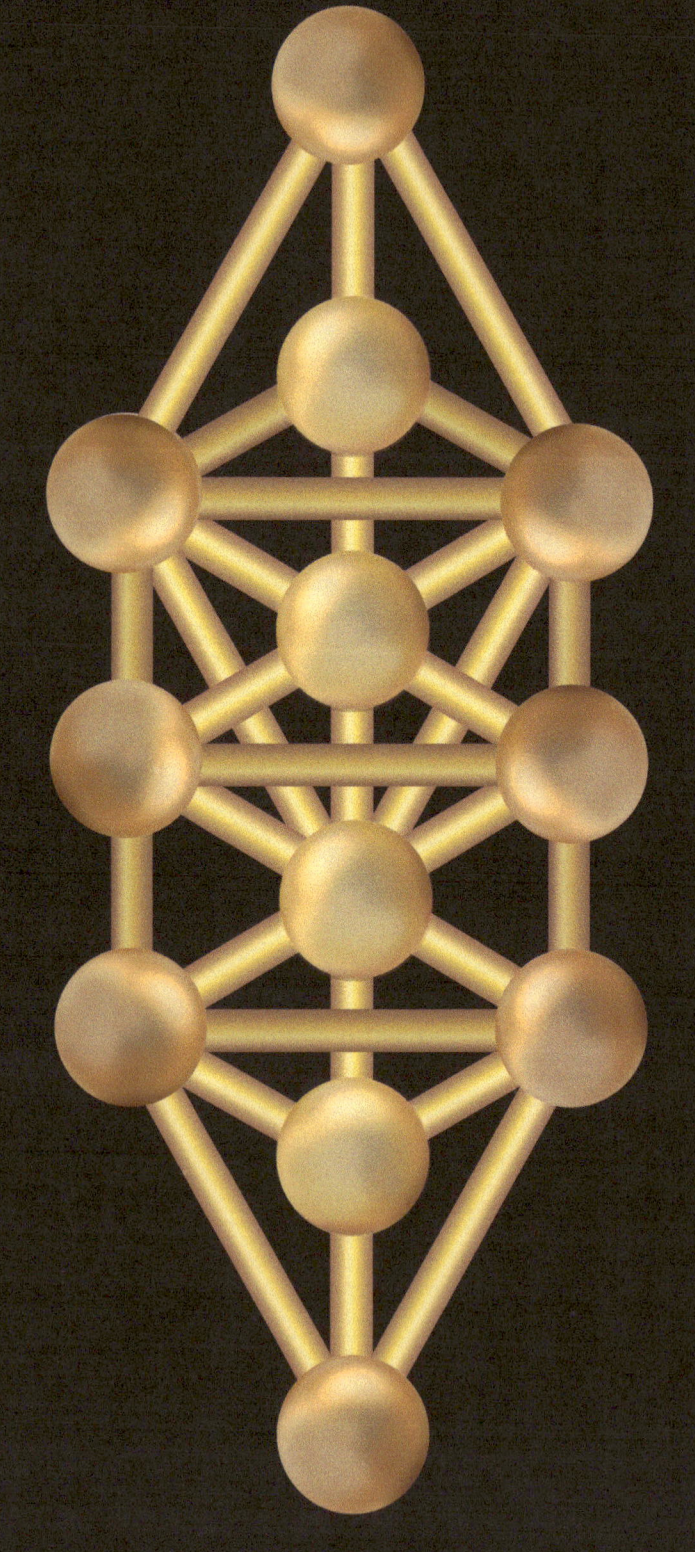

## A Pause for Thought

The twelfth Sephira

Each pathway and each Sephira resonates and sings with its own voice, its own unique musical note. The twenty-two letters create a harmony that is reflected in ancient music, the twenty-two notes familiar to us in the Indian musical scale. With the recognition of the twelfth Sephira, the twelve gates of Jerusalem, we can hear all the notes of the chromatic scale.

This leads us to observe that in three dimensions, new sounds, new letters and new vibrations are born.

Every aspect of the Sephirotic Tree revolves gracefully, sings eloquently and performs an infinite myriad creation of holographic worlds. Each vortex of light creates a nucleus that gives birth to perpetual matrices of reality. The light overflows from each Sephira, unfolding a graceful and mathematically poetic twist, an about turn, of numbers that replay the DNA twist, written within every living thing.

We see this code within the mathematical possibilities of each Sephira and each pathway. By adding together, the numbers of each pathway, we see that the precise moment the numbers of the Sephira delicately twist, the pathways replicate the movement, and all begins its descent into the physical planes of existence.

And God saw that it was good

# The Destiny of the Physical Universe and Humanity's role in Creation

The minute instant of the nucleus of light coming into being, of the force of focus and momentum, causes the first ripple, the first precession. This is the result of the "pebble in water", this result, this natural reaction, is the recognition, the acceptance, the realisation of the nucleus. This is the primal "emotion" or soul, the formulation of the Sephira. This receptivity is that which accepts and assesses the creation of the nucleus, the name of God. So God "saw" that it was good. This natural reaction is the primal emotion of recognition of being.

So, each and every minutiae of life, is understood as being alive by the recognition of the soul, or, in simple terms, "emotion". The instant a baby takes the first breath it is followed instantaneously by the recognition or emotion of being alive. This is observance. That instant of awareness, of living itself, whether that be in a simple form, like that of a plant photosynthesising, or an animal taking its first breath, or simply the reaction of an atom to being observed is the fractal repetition of "seeing" that it is good. This is the entire reality of every aspect of that which we understand as life.

As humans we are the fulfilment of this. We assess by emotion the reality and existence of all.

It is easy to understand the importance of every realisation of physical, life; the minute chance of this existence, the fleeting chance of even an amoeba achieving physical life in comparison to the immensity we observe in the night sky, is unique. Consider just for a few minutes the immensity of the universe that we comprehend. Consider the infinite myriad stars. Consider the one in trillions chance that you are alive at all. The evolution of every aspect of life is so rare, so exceptional, to have developed as far as a human being is fantastic and extraordinary. Even if you believe this to be the random result of chaotic chance, you would have to concede that the evolution of the planet Earth and of every countless life form is extraordinary. Each human life is more than extraordinary, it is unique, it is vital and it is profound.

When we look further into the life of a human being and see that it exists only to a small degree in the physical world and that its existence is recognised in the world of imagination, in the world of thoughts and in the world of feelings, we can truly begin to understand humanity as the bridge between the many dimensions of reality. We can begin to understand the role of each human being as the ultimate image of the creator, as creators and the ultimate potential of imagination. Each and every atom is the continual Birth of God. Each and every human being is the unfolding of imagination and the constant and infinite Birth of God.

Let us revisit the process.

It is difficult for the human to accept that all these aspects of creation are eternal and have no beginning. Our minds demand a starting point and even an ending point; this is the physical limitation of our own lives. It is vital to grasp that every aspect, "stage" or process is in itself infinite, constant and eternal.

The formulation of what we call God dwells within the infinite state of Ain, within Ain is the eternal formulation of the recognition of "nothing", separating it and recognising from the potential of "all" Ain Soph. The two interconnected states are endless and immersed within themselves. These are the two polarities. Receptive and Emissive. This causes movement. Movement against the eternal stillness of Ain, causes friction which results in ignition. This is the illumination, the essence and creation of light, Ain Soph Aur.

The immense and eternal light gathers momentum. Its only course is to gather speed, to whip up an infinite vortex of ever intensifying light. This is the process of implosion. The immeasurable energy of the ever intensifying light, that appears to create a vortex of light within the eternal immersion of light Ain Soph Aur.

This cone of spinning light appears to formulate a pin point of infinite and absolute light; This eternal fraction of intensity is the moment of complete recognition. The moment of coming into being, the constant instant of Ehieh, "I will be".

This instant begins another process of eternal formulation. The drop of a pebble into water.

A constant ebb of movement, light, creating rings of energy flowing from the pinnacle of perfect contact. This is caused by the initial spinning vortex, whipping up the frequency and intensity of light, so that the moment of the internal pin point of light is a higher and infinitely faster frequency than the light from whence it came and within which it exists.

These rings of energy formulate as they reverberate against and within the boundary of light that resonates at a different frequency.

The intense speed of this original process sends the energy into propulsion. Imagine the process of a pinball machine. The ball is rocketed forward and rebounds from side to side; this pinball of intense light, ricochets against the boundary of the light of Ain Soph Aur.

Each point of contact creates another nucleus of intense light and from it flows rings of energy, that formulate and stabilise, by rebounding against the light of Ain Soph Aur. This is the lightening flash, the first primeval Tree of Light.

As each formulation becomes "over full" overwhelmed and only able to receive, it shatters. This eternal shattering, sends out immeasurable frequency that draws back into itself, and reformulates, stabilising and completing the process of natural ebb and flow. Each aspect becomes stable and permanent, allowing the receptive and emissive process to create a continuum.

The energy is reinforced during this process, static geometrical force, compounded by the repetition of energetic force. Pathways of stable light commune and connect each pin point of light and precession.

It is imperative to reconcile your thoughts to each and every process being infinite, eternal and constant.

At each point of contact, another Tree of Light process bursts into being. A holographic, infinite and eternal creation of light and life.

Each and every instant is a process of recognition, illumination, light recognising its own reality and birth.

Birth recognising its existence. The moment of birth recognising its own consciousness. Infinite recognition, and infinite creation.

All eternal and constant, continual and permanent instants of infinite recognition.

The DNA twist and time

The elegant poetry of the numbers, the sound impulses that compound and manifest the dimensions which gravitate into physical, tangible creation, repeat, in fractal, ever diminishing patterns. We can see the beautiful DNA twist, the about turn that the numbers make in the middle of the Tree of Life. As they approach Sephira Tiphareth and as they flow from it, the graceful "about turn" that changes in perfect harmony the order in which they appear. This we can equate to the constant twist in the DNA structure itself. We can also recognise the constant ellipse that flows through the Tree of Life. Observing this and the numbers that flow within it, we can see that the appearance time itself is suspended within the structure; we can see that this infinite and constant state appears only as time from our small glimpse within the ellipse, that which appears closest to our physical reality. The ever evolving universe and the precise dance of the cosmos, reveals to us that at times, certain crossover points in the ellipse seem closer than at others, according to the planet Earth's momentum. Hence superstition tells us that the "veil" is thinner at certain times of the year. We see only a small fraction of the permanent ellipse that we call time, which appears to be linear, in our experience. All things are relevant to the moment and perspective from which they are observed. The ellipse is also constant, that which was, is and will be, all at the same time; we are all that was, is and will be in exactly the same way.

We see the imprint of time and memory within physical DNA, we can trace the source of generations within it. Genetic memory lies hidden within DNA, this is image of time within biology.

In the cosmos, black holes are the physical expression of this mathematical ellipse. Within a black hole the entire formula is displayed; the poetic 'DNA' journey of divine mathematics and the eternal illusion of time both combine. The voyage into a black hole is one of transformation, that precisely replicates the journey of the numbers of the Sephirotic Tree.

# A Pause for Thought

It is therefore a conclusion that there is no "Divine" plan. That there is only the absolute law of cause and effect. This law is indeed absolute. The entirety of creation on every conceivable level and dimension is a result of perfect logic. The law of cause and effect is the law of precise and perfect logical progression. Each and every reaction and formulation is the result of absolute logic and nothing strays from this law, ever.

Let us now contemplate the whole wondrous vista of creation. Each and every moment is an infinite, perpetual, and a constant of creation, the eternal Birth of God.

All creation, having its essence in the limitless state of Ain, Limitless Nothing is its own recognition of nothingness. Existing only and utterly, because in order for it to exist it must be recognised by its opposite, Limitless something. Limitless something can only exist in the recognition of Limitless Nothing.

All things exist only because of their own non existence.

Within Ain is the essence of all things, the beginning and precursor of emission. Positive force, that expresses itself as the force to move.

The result of Nothing plus movement, creates friction. Positive against negative, creating friction that causes ignition. This is the wondrous moment of the creation of sublime light, Ain Soph Aur.

This is the essence of all that is concealed within the phrase 'Let there be light'.

This is all that propels the journey of absolute logic. The progression of one phase determines the only logical response to itself.

Every phase and creation, response and reverberation is permanent and eternal.

Each nucleus of utter light is formed in a constant state of formation. Each propels through its own coming into being; a process of self recognition, precession; waves of light energy, followed by the self recognition of sound reverberation.

Each nucleus creates, as a response, its own infinite journey of creation; creating into being an infinite and perpetual formation of endless Tree of Life matrices, hurtling on, in a holographic, infinite state of limitless creation.

Each Tree of Life caught up in an endless momentum of movement. Gracefully spinning, poetically performing the elegant DNA twist in its centrifugal point. The perfect light that condenses within Tifaret, the centrifugal point, does its mathematical about turn and delivers the light into the rays of the visible light spectrum.

As the numbers allow this reversal of energy, the prism reveals the physical, visible light spectrum, that we experience as seeing and being seen. That we experience as physical reality.

And onwards the eternal journey of

immeasurable creation, constant movement, graceful spinning and dancing, an effortless and endless repetition of events and mathematical verification, until the minutiae of the journey of utter logic, presents as the tiny world of the quantum dance, the world of atoms and the most minute of all creation.

Humans, made of this beautiful and infinite creation, experience at last their own place in the laws of magnetic attraction and understand their ability to harness and to consciously become the creators of new and infinite universes.

# Gravity and Quantum Reality

The laws of the universe are exact and absolute. Each and every force in the universe is the result of logical progression. Nothing deviates from this.

Gravitational waves are the same force that governs the momentum of the quantum, minute dance of life.

This can be traced back to the origins of movement, that lie is a state of constant ebbing within the infinite Ayn Soph; this in turn have their existence in the non manifest, nothingness of Ayn.

This original force of movement that we have studied is replicated within the infinite creation of the Sephirot and at every point of discovery and self recognition of the creator, as infinite Trees of Life are born.

The physical universe that we experience lies within Malkuth, the logical culmination of the immense force of movement, the waves of gravity. This is our experience of planets in their eternal cosmic dance; all spinning themselves and taking part in their effortless progress around the sun.

The force of movement is immeasurable and can be equated to the same effect of plucking the string of an instrument. The origin, the first pluck of the string is the instigator and is far stronger than the effect. The effect is the much faster vibration of the string that reverberates and answers with a musical note. The quantum world vibrates with far more intensity and speed, as it is result of the original 'pluck of the string'. It appears chaotic only because the vibration is too fast for us to detect the rhythm.

Hence our experience of the physical world appearing to be solid; atoms formulating what appears to be solid, but in reality are all playing their separate roles in this cosmic dance of response to absolute logic.

An atom is the most minute manifestation of self recognition. Its physical existence and expression of reality is created by momentum. The components dancing around each other, bound up within momentum. The positive and negative components reveal the primal states of non-being and being, recognised by its own negative and positive natures. The primal phases are expressed by the three components; the creator in three: protons, neutrons and electrons, behaving in this way.

Dark matter is essential to the formation of the physical universe. It is the natural essence of nothing, the development of the original Ayn, that contains within it the possibility of movement and therefore light and life. Dark matter is the background and container of life, in Malkuth, the physical and most intense of the great, eternal dance of life. All things have their existence within nothing. Movement is the result of the recognition of eternal nothing. Life is created by movement. Movement and thought are one and the same. Movement propels thought on an ever unfolding journey of coming into awareness. Awareness develops into consciousness. Consciousness develops and becomes intention. Thought is the essence of life and the quintessence of all creation.

Thought is the force of life. The infinite journey of constantly developing thought, that recognises itself in what we describe as emotion, or resonance, or response. Begins its voyage of discovery in vast eddies of movement; waves and spins way beyond human comprehension, and human ability to 'scientifically' detect their immensity. This can be illustrated by the action of plucking a string on an instrument. The initial force is great and results in the much faster vibration of the string, which results in sound. There is no conflict between the huge force of gravitational waves, resulting in the minute dance of the quantum world. This can only be reconciled by seeing the story of creation as a whole interwoven, journey of logic. The 'plucker of the string' is logic itself, resulting from primal nothingness. The result is the 'plucker of the string', movement itself, can only be described as the primal, unformed thought. Primal movement begins the first immense vortex of spinning energy that formulates an illusion of the nucleus of being. This is the beginning; the Birth of God.

Thought is life, expressed through the creation of light and energy. Light is the recognition of life or reality. Visible light is the journey of life in what we describe as the physical universe.

Light is the living spirit of life; all thought is alive. All thought has no choice but to create a result and all thought has a destination. All destinations propel another force of creation and are connected to all thought and all recognition; ever onwards within infinity.

Mathematics and numbers are the unfolding states of movement and self recognition. Movement is the force that unfolds infinite direction and the infinite, elegantly simple development of dimension. Movement is the energy of stability and the provider of the illusion of structure.

There is no death; there is only change.

The human consciousness is based upon hope; even the ultimate act of suicide is an act of hope; the hope of escape into something better, even if that is a belief in an unconscious and never ending personal sleep. As humanity begins to grow up, the idea of a 'humanised' God, meeting out punishment and retribution is rejected. Old ideas of religion, old ideas of economics and politics will be rejected and this primeval state of humanity will be looked back upon by future generations as we now look back on the dinosaurs.

From the immense to the imperceptible; from the initial immeasurable, eternal waves that bring about the constant implosion of light;

to the minute and barely measurable world of atoms, neutrinos, integral and semi integral spins, the entire dazzling journey of thought; all without exception lives and is a result of the law of cause and effect; the law of divine logic.

Humanity is a vital result of this journey. Every thought, compounded by emotion is alive. Every thought creates its own universe. As the human grows up, through the voyage of many incarnations, the rising awareness of the divine power of creation and the power of thought begins to awaken. The unending possibilities that this reveals is wondrous.

Every single atom of life is the constant, infinite and eternal Birth of God.

Each atom, each particle, every tiny, minute aspect of life is the ever developing awareness of the creator. All life, whether it be a plant, an animal or a human being, is the eternal developing awareness of the creator.

The primal movement within Ain Sof is the key of physical life. All things, even the most apparently static object is alive; it is alive because it is made up of atoms that are constantly moving. There is no solid creation without movement. Movement is the life force, which is the one source of the creator. We are only able to 'see' and experience the physical world because everything, without exception, is made up of moving atoms. Everything in the physical realm is alive and is part of the force of life.

# Incarnation

A spirit, an expression of the consciousness of God, chooses to begin and to continue to participate in its own evolutionary journey as a creator on the planet Earth because the physical universe and the planet Earth itself is the ultimate accumulation of the force of creation. The planet Earth is the 'perfection story' of the evolution of logic and is the perfect observation of seeing and being seen. The human is the best development of needing to see physicality. The Earth provides the physical experiences of seeing and being seen. For the human it is the visible classroom of learning the laws of creation, of cause and effect and the magnetic law of attraction, which are absolute. For the fulfilment of the ultimate human destiny as the conscious creator by thought, the physical Earth is the perfect teacher.

This is the intense focus of the energies of the infinite dimensions of the Tree of Life. Malkuth, the Kingdom, the physical universe, is the conclusion and condensation of the previous energies and dimensions. The physical universe in turn, by existing, creates infinite, holographic universes.

To envisage the entirety of the voyage of discovery, which is the journey of life in myriad forms, we must contemplate all things existing within Ayn, infinite nothing. Within this, exists recognition of nothingness which is existence itself, Ayn Sof. Within Ayn Sof is the movement that causes friction, which cause the implosion of light. The whirling vortex creates what appears, due to the speed, to be the first nucleus of light. This then sets off the process of precession and recognition of being.

As each nucleus comes into being an infinite journey of Tree of Life matrices are born. Each new nucleus creates a never ending holographic creating of infinite Sephirotic Trees. Each new nucleus becomes a more intensified experience and a more intense recognition of its own essence. It becomes more of its own self.

Our own universe, Malkuth, the creator of endless universes, resides within and is the result of the limitless Tree of Life, self generating and self creating matrix of divine mathematics and divine eternity. Our own universe endlessly and eternally expands and creates new matrices of energy and new universes.

The whole immense holographic creation is an infinite vibrating voyage of endless discovery. A voyage of discovery which has eternal beginnings and that can never end.

All things exist in the present, forever. All exists within Ayn, within Ayn Sof, within the wondrous implosion of light, Ayn Sof Aur. All things exist within the eternal holographic Tree of Life and are the eternal and infinite creation.

From the eternal and the infinite, from the immense, to the minute atomic world, everything conceivable and all that is yet to be conceived, is alive; created within the immeasurable, perpetual dance, reverberating in a growing awareness of being. Forever a unique experience and forever part of the creator.

The meaning of life is creation. The meaning of creation is Life. This is the eternal and infinite Birth of God.